COLLECTED WORKS OF
CHARLES BERG

Volume 3

# THE UNCONSCIOUS
# SIGNIFICANCE OF HAIR

# THE UNCONSCIOUS
# SIGNIFICANCE OF HAIR

CHARLES BERG

Routledge
Taylor & Francis Group

LONDON AND NEW YORK

First published in 1951 by George Allen & Unwin Ltd

This edition first published in 2022
by Routledge
4 Park Square, Milton Park, Abingdon, Oxon OX14 4RN

and by Routledge
605 Third Avenue, New York, NY 10158

*Routledge is an imprint of the Taylor & Francis Group, an informa business*

*British Library Cataloguing in Publication Data*
A catalogue record for this book is available from the British Library

ISBN: 978-1-032-16970-5 (Set)
ISBN: 978-1-003-25348-8 (Set) (ebk)
ISBN: 978-1-032-17051-0 (Volume 3) (hbk)
ISBN: 978-1-032-17062-6 (Volume 3) (pbk)
ISBN: 978-1-003-25159-0 (Volume 3) (ebk)

DOI: 10.4324/9781003251590

**Publisher's Note**
The publisher has gone to great lengths to ensure the quality of this reprint but points out that some imperfections in the original copies may be apparent.

**Disclaimer**
The publisher has made every effort to trace copyright holders and would welcome correspondence from those they have been unable to trace.

This book is a re-issue originally published in 1948. The language used is a reflection of its era and no offence is meant by the Publishers to any reader by this re-publication.

# THE UNCONSCIOUS SIGNIFICANCE OF HAIR

By CHARLES BERG

M.D.(LOND.), D.P.M.

*Fellow of the British Psychological Society*

*Consulting Psychiatrist to the British Hospital for Functional Nervous Disorders*

*Late Physician to the Institute for the Scientific Treatment of Delinquency and the Tavistock Clinic*

*London*

GEORGE ALLEN & UNWIN LTD

RUSKIN HOUSE MUSEUM STREET

PRINTED IN GREAT BRITAIN
*in* 12-*point Garamond type*
BY THE BLACKFRIARS PRESS LTD.
SMITH-DORRIEN ROAD, LEICESTER

# *Preface*

THIS book is really a psychiatric criticism of normality based upon a chosen item of typically normal behaviour. Its implications are far wider and deeper than the title suggests.

Hair-activities are chosen merely as a sample of uncritically accepted human behaviour. On examining them in the light of dreams, anthropology, folklore, symptoms and perversions, they are shown to be an expression of instinct-driven tensions and conflicts. The popular illusion that they are determined by reason or adaptation to reality is exploded.

The corollary is inescapable : if in this innocent particular our thoughts and behaviour are symptomatic expressions of an unconscious conflict or complex, how much more psychopathic would our more significant ideas, beliefs, institutions, customs and laws prove to be on similar detailed investigation ! Is, therefore, our self-expression in life and civilisation nothing more than a symptom, identical in its source and mechanism with the symptoms of nervous and mental illness ?

I am indebted to the editors of the *International Journal of Psycho-Analysis* for permission to incorporate the material of my paper published in Vol. XVII, Part I, of their Journal.

CHARLES BERG

HARLEY STREET,
LONDON, W.1

*September,* 1950

▼

# CONTENTS

# SECTION I

# *Introductory*

THE attempt to distinguish between Reality factors (Reality principle) and Emotional factors (Pleasure-pain principle) in assessing the cause of behaviour is not above criticism. Apart from the philosophic objection that we do not know what reality is, or (as modern psychology would put it) that the reality we seem to know is determined by the selective function of our emotional interests, there remains the evident truth that emotional values are also realities *for us*, albeit psychological or subjective realities.

They, or their instinctive bases, are real enough to demand consideration, and some degree of obedience, if we would preserve mental and physical health, and individual and racial survival.

Nevertheless, it is sometimes useful to examine behaviour in the light of this arbitrary distinction (between Reality values and Emotional values), if only to correct the naïve assumption that behaviour is a response to the demands of environmental reality ; that it is necessary, reasonable and logical.

Whereas it is generally recognised that psychotic or symptomatic behaviour has relatively little reality causation, and must therefore be activated by endopsychic tensions, typically normal behaviour, on the other hand, is readily assumed, even by some psychologists, to be amply conditioned by the demands of environmental reality.

It would seem at *first* sight, that *normal* behaviour *is* primarily a response to reality demands and that this is its essential distinction from morbid behaviour. Closer examination however is apt to reveal that even the most typically normal of all normal behaviour (e.g., our daily habits of dress[1] and toilet) has its real cause or source in endopsychic tension. The most that can be said for it on behalf of the Reality principle, is that it does not so seriously interfere with our adjustment to reality as to menace survival.

The attempt that is made to explain normal behaviour as a logical consequence of reality demands has the defensive advantage of tacitly, or tactfully, ignoring its instinctive basis. The process may be called 'rationalisation', the defensive importance of which was originally emphasised by Ernest Jones. It serves the purpose of concealing or disguising the essential cause, the real source, of behaviour as the release of endopsychic tension. It paves the way for many popular errors, such as the belief that the behaviour of the abnormal (neurotic or psychotic) is inexplicable and of a totally different nature from the behaviour of normal, reasonable human beings. Meanwhile these latter may pursue their established habits unconscious of the existence within them of the instinctive forces from which these habits have their source.

In this monograph I would insist only that, as in the general theory of psycho-analysis, the term 'unconscious' be recognised as really meaning unconscious, i.e., not ordinarily accessible to consciousness. The discovery of what lies in the unconscious is made possible only by analytical technique, such as free-associations of thought under analytical conditions, dream analysis, transference and transference analysis. Discoveries so made are not legitimate matter for assessment by conscious levels of mental functioning. And this should be recognised. We do not presume to subject the findings of astronomers,[2] physicists or microscopists (who have used special instruments with which to make their discoveries) to the critical rejection of our 'common sense'. The dis-

[1] Cf. J. C. Flugel: *The Psychology of Clothes.*

[2] Though it is less than four centuries since Galileo was imprisoned and nearly executed by the Church for discovering that the earth was round.

2

coveries of the analyst are even less meet for conscious-level assessment : for, generally speaking, the material of the unconscious is unconscious just because *it has already been rejected* by consciousness as unwelcome, and continues to be resisted by it.

There is, of course, no harm in examining normal, as well as abnormal, behaviour and beliefs in the light of unconscious material ; indeed, the explanation of psychogenic symptoms is made possible only by this means. The thesis of this book is that even the most commonplace and normal human behaviour similarly has its essential source in the unconscious and similarly can be explained adequately only in the light of this source. To illustrate this a specific example is chosen, namely our behaviour and attitudes in regard to hair.

# Normal Hair-Behaviour

NATURE has endowed man with hair all over the surface of his body (with a few exceptions, such as palms of hands, and soles of feet) growing in some places sparsely, and in others more abundantly. Amongst the more densely hairy regions there are two that are commonly displayed in his clothed state, namely his head and the lower part of his face. It is noteworthy that it is these regions which are visible to his fellows that alone concern him.

Throughout the ages, from the most primitive times of which we have any record, man has devoted a considerable portion of his daily life to some form of interference with his hair. Either he is making it seem longer, or more abundant than it really is, or else he is cutting it off and making it seem less than it really is, or else (as in shaving) he is endeavouring to remove every trace of it.

We need not waste our time with a tedious recital of coiffures, shampooings, scentings, wavings, curlings, singeings, greasings, dyeings, eyebrow pluckings, and suchlike ; nor with artificial contraptions such as combs, crowns, garlands, and hats which are used either to exhibit or to conceal hair. We need not review the evolution from natural beards, muttonchop whiskers, waxed moustaches and so on to the modern preference for the clean shave. I shall merely call attention to the fact that this hair behaviour has in women become so important that it has been specialised and relegated to a host of professionals. In London there are 3,500 registered hairdressing establishments and 8,000 registered professional hairdressers.[1] As long as seventeen

[1]Figures supplied by the London County Council and based upon the census returns of 1931.

4

years ago a newspaper[1] stated that thirty million pounds a year was being spent by women on permanent waving alone.

Woman does not rest content with this systematic delegation of her duty. She is herself constantly doing something to her hair. She even carries a little mirror everywhere with her with the principal object of looking at her hair to see that it is all right. Obviously it is a source of anxiety to her. She cannot feel right unless she is sure her hair is right ; but it seems she can never feel *quite* sure that it is right—she must have another look in her mirror. To quote Vivian Meik : 'No daughter of Eve has ever yet lived who has never caressed her hair. The women of Borneo, of Brazil on the upper reaches of the Amazon, at the source of the Zambezi—from Eve in Eden to the vanity-sodden clients of a Mayfair beauty parlour—all, without exception, at some time or other yield homage to their hair.'[2]

Clearly hair is of enormous importance. We are never indifferent to it in human beings or even in animals. Its presence or absence, its length, texture, curl, colour, all have their effect upon us and influence our likes and dislikes and our judgments. Even verbal references to hair do not find us indifferent. This is borne out by the numerous popular phrases and comic songs in which the reference to 'hair' seems to release a disproportionate quantity of emotional reaction. It is evident that some source of libidinal tension is being tapped by such simple references to hair.[3] We smile when told that certain edible wares will make our hair curl. There are a host of phrases such as : 'There's hair' ; 'Get your hair cut' ; or the threat 'I'll cut your hair' ; 'Keep your hair on.' The word 'hairy' is sometimes used as an expression of contempt.

The significance of the colour of the hair is introduced

[1] *The Daily Herald,* 5th May, 1932.
[2] Vivian Meik, *The People of the Leaves,* page 35.
[3] In keeping with the principles laid down in Freud's *Wit and the Unconscious.*

in the old song and jibe : 'Ginger, you're barmy.' It seems to denote some unconscious association between red hair and barminess. Is this a recognition that excessive libidinal energy may overthrow ego control ? Similarly there was a song : 'Captain Ginger, O.T. 'ot', and so on. No doubt many other phrases will occur to the reader.

To get back to our presumably sane preoccupations and activities with hair : we may now ask the question, what are the causes for this behaviour ? Does reality demand that we should behave like this ?

The primary advantage is perhaps that of keeping our hair out of our eyes and out of the way of our activities. Similarly, hair that grows about the mouth is kept out of our food, and is prevented from collecting our nasal and oral secretions.

If any should consider that this is a sufficient reality advantage to justify its removal by shaving he should reflect that the pubic hair, at least in women, is subject to similar disadvantages, but the world seems to get on very well without a daily shaving in that region.[1][2][3]

Secondary or cultural advantages are those of conforming to the social order of things ; but I would point out that though such advantages might be important in explaining any *individual's* hair activities, they do not explain the hair activities of society as a whole. They do not explain why such a custom as shaving should come about, nor why it should be maintained for so long even as the last few decades. The problem is still unanswered as to why this social custom exists.

[1] Greek women used to shave the pubic hair—as in Greek sculpture and in art.
[2] Police criterion of obscenity in photography of women is visibility of pubic hair.
[3] With regard to the paying of conscious attention to one's pubic hair, there is probably censorship or taboo at work, similar to that which, more particularly in the saints and religious persons, prevents them from paying ordinary hygienic attention to their genital organs. For example, it is said of Thomas à Becket that it was only when his vestments were removed after his death that it was discovered what a truly holy man he was. This censorship or taboo does not operate in regard to the head and facial hair.

We may well ask what would happen if we entirely ignored our hair or adopted a strictly reality attitude towards it. Perhaps when it got in our way we would hurriedly cut off any such parts as did get in our way. I think of the Indian fakirs, and it seems to me possible that it would become so matted as to give us no trouble at all, apart perhaps from the satisfaction of an occasional scratch.

Now the reality disadvantages comprise a more formidable list. They could be classified under time, energy and expense. That valuable ten minutes of every morning when we are fresh and capable of our best work is used up in the painstaking and exacting task of shaving, only to be repeated twenty-four hours later. In a life of sixty adult years the time devoted to the morning shave alone amounts to 3,652½ hours, or 152 days nearly one-half of a year. A disadvantage not to be ignored is that of daily damage to the skin, and the risk of accidents, which ever and anon materialise in the form of cuts, sores, pimples, skin infections, and other misfortunes.

I said something about cost when I mentioned thirty million pounds yearly on permanent waving alone. There is also the cost of a variety of apparatus, both individual and professional. I said there were 3,500 hairdressing establishments in London. This is confirmed by the Hairdressers' Registration Council as recently as October, 1949, but the Incorporated Guild of Hairdressers, Wigmakers and Perfumers writes me (October, 1949): 'A reasonable estimate of the hairdressing establishments [presumably registered and unregistered] in the Metropolitan Police Area would be 10,000.' The Hulton Survey of the hairdressing and beauty trades published in May, 1948, gives the number of hairdressing shops in Great Britain as 35,200. I feel that all these figures are probably an underestimate as there is no means of assessing the number of unregistered establishments. *The Hairdressers' Weekly Journal,* of Frith Street, Soho, used to have a mailing list of over 20,000 in the United Kingdom to whom their journal was circulated every week, and one would not think that hairdressers were a particularly journalistic class.

# SECTION III

# Clinical Evidence of the
# Unconscious Significance of Hair

In the realms of organic medicine it is usual to state actual observations, clinical, laboratory, or pathological. For example, we do not substitute for these summaries or generalisations. We describe the actual position of the apex beat, the exact details of the blood count, and so forth.

Now in psychological medicine the only facts we have corresponding to these are the actual verbatim statements and behaviour of the patient during the analytical session. These, I feel, should be regarded as data of observation of the first magnitude. They are our facts, and occupy a privileged position to which theories, however plausible, cannot lay claim. My impression is that theories are commonly these facts (the verbatim statements of patients) subjected to the various Ego and Super-ego modifications of the analyst or theorist. They are commonly watered down by the usual censoring apparatus.

I therefore propose to put before you a few facts : the actual words and behaviour of certain patients under analysis, with as little abbreviation as possible.

First of all we will consider a few dreams from a number of different cases.

The first analysand dreams as follows :

'I was sitting in a bus close beside a young woman with brilliant red hair. I put my hand on her head and pressed her hair and experienced feelings of *great pleasure*.'

His associations of thought :

'I don't know anyone with red hair like this girl had. My girl has fair, golden hair.'

9

At this point he suddenly flushes up and becomes silent.
He confesses :

'The other day I succeeded in exposing her pubic region
and was delighted to find that her pubic hair had a distinct
reddish tinge. I laughed and called it "Ginger nob" and put
my hand on it—just as I had put my hand on the girl's head
in the dream. I have only *just* thought of this.'

I quote this dream as a simple and clear example of displacement upwards from the pubic hair to the hair of the
head.

It seems at first sight rather fortuitous that this patient
linked up the activity of his dream, pressing the hair of a
red head, to a recent sexual experience, but, as he himself
was the first to say, the real link lay in the *identity* of the
*emotion* which accompanied the acts in the two instances.

Here is an observation of first-rate importance. We see
*in statu nascendi* the operation of the mechanism of displacement upwards. Even one first-hand observation of this
mechanism in operation cannot be ignored. There is no
alternative to the acceptance of this as a psychological fact.
Specifically we see the affect or emotion pertaining to the
pubic hair directly and distinctly displaced on to the hair of
the head.

It still remains to be shown what affect, or conflicting
affects, pertain to the pubic hair, and why. For the moment
we will leave that question and proceed to another dream,
this time the dream of a patient of a very different character.

He dreams as follows :

'You (the analyst) were rubbing some stuff into my hair
—like a white lather of soap. My mother was there and was
very anxious to help.'

I asked what my rubbing of his hair might mean.

He said :

'Well, I suppose you might be curing me—for that is
what I am here for, and what you are here for. Curing me

means making me normal sexually.' (His sexual life is limited to homosexual phantasy.)

A. 'This white lather of soap?'

P. Silence. Then he laughs and says, 'I had a ridiculous thought just now. I thought of semen.'

At the next session the patient says:

'I have been thinking about the dream. I will try to remember the theory I arrived at. The first thought that came to me was that you may have been cutting my hair; but it was not you, it was my father that wanted my hair cut shorter. I used to hate it.'

(Most children at some stage cry very much at having their hair cut.)

'You were doing the reverse—making it grow.

'Now I have my hair as I want it—not too short. I thought my father noticed this the other day when I visited him and I thought to myself: "He can go to hell".

'I have thought that you were restoring my hair in the dream. Treating it in some way . . . And now I remember that my hair was *short* . . . shorter than I ever have it nowadays. I have a feeling that it had something to do with my illness. Short hair is in the nature of a castration. It is part of discipline. In the army hair is cut short, and the same in prisons. Monks used to shave the head completely.

'In the dream the emotion of anxiety was my mother's, but it actually indicates *my* real emotions and anxiety about the analysis. I keep thinking, "How can I get some progress? How can I get better?" I suppose it really means how can I get normal sexually? How can I get my penis back? You are helping me to get it back. That, of course, is what you are doing in the dream. Rubbing my hair to make it grow. The white lather, of course, is semen. The short hair is the castrated penis which is being restored by you through the analysis. (It reaches a stage where it could emit semen.)'

A third analysand dreams as follows:

'I had my hair cut and somebody (a lady, I think) re-marked that it was very nice. Then I went out and had it done again. The barber cut off the same amount again. As a result it was very short. I put plenty of grease on it and plastered it down. People thought it looked absurd and laughed at it.'

Later on it transpires that the most striking thing about this dream was the nature of the second hair cut, or rather the result thereof. It was that the head was left with several avenues of complete baldness. The avenues ran parallel from the forehead to the back of the head. Each avenue was one inch wide and four inches or five inches long. They were separated from each other by a single row of single hairs. These rows of single-file hairs stood erect, one inch high, and separated the hair-free avenues. Each of these latter was therefore, one inch wide by one inch deep by four or five inches long. It was these erect hairs that the dreamer care-fully brushed down flat to cover the avenues of baldness. He was at some pains to do this.

His associations to this dream are so voluminous that I shall have to select and condense, although the result will be that we shall not do justice to this very striking dream.

Briefly, the woman is the mother. The haircut pleased her. So he went a step further and had still more cut. He says :

'I have brushed down what was left for the same reason. Smooth and sleek like a lounge lizard, to please the woman. I think I must have some sort of ideal woman in my mind.' (The ideal woman is the mother, to achieve whose love he must discard the penis.)

With regard to haircut in general he says :

'Haircut is conforming to an ideal that civilisation has built up. Haircut, like other civilised acts, is the desire to conceal the nakedness of emotions and desires in order to please somebody.'

Other remarks of his are as follows :

'I don't like to see hair standing up on end.'

He then remembers a man he knows whose hair stands on end, and whom he dislikes for this reason.

He says :

'He is a gay dog, especially with the opposite sex. I was just the reverse of this type.

'In the dream after the second haircut I became an object of ridicule ; and that is what I am at the present stage of my life when I cannot enter into the fun of things and cannot find a word to say if there is a girl about. I am in a ridiculous position.'

Going back to his thoughts he continues to voice his objections to erect hair :

'It is rather a low-down business to have erect hair. Not the sort of hair that stamps a member of the upper classes. Makes me think of the "Bill Sykes" type of individual—anti-social.

'Although there is no connection, I think of an incident as a kid. I took a cheap seat at a cinema. In the darkness I heard a noise—a drip-drip, and I could make out it was from some women in front relieving themselves on the floor. I was repulsed. A foul type of humanity—a stage between animal and human. The thought is of their genital organs and of their pubic hair.

'I suppose the association to hair is really pubic hair. And to the erect hair—anti-social—the bold, bad penis. Erect penis is not tolerated by society, it is anti-social like erect hair. I might not please a woman with a perfectly erect penis. I would plaster it down like I did the erect hair. I would hide the fact and control the desire. Desire is invariably manifested by an erect penis.

'The idea of having to have less hair (second haircut) reminds me of the idea that I ought to have less penis. As a boy my elder brother once remarked what a big penis I had.

'Oh ! well, I see more or less what the dream is about.

I don't like my hair for the same reason that I didn't like the erect hair or the erect penis. It was *rude*, so I had it cut and the woman was pleased. I wanted to please her so much more that I went too far and ended up in this ridiculous state of almost complete baldness.

'I tried to get back to a state of normality or to an appearance thereof by plastering down the rude erect hairs and at the same time covering the ridiculous avenues of baldness.

'These bald avenues (one inch wide and one inch deep by four or five inches long) are the shape and size of a penis. They are the places from which the penis had been removed. They are as ridiculous and laughable as the erect hair between them is rude and anti-social. My plastering the erect hair down did away with the rudeness, at the same time as it covered the ridiculous nudity.'

It is easy to see here the conflict between genital libido in the form of retention or exhibition of the penis on the one hand and super-ego-instigated castration on the other. A compromise solution is arrived at by means of plastering down the hair.

It is unnecessary for me to call attention to the relation-ship between this patient's associations to his dream and the usual social behaviour towards hair. We are all familiar with the objection to erect hair. We are all familiar with the tendency to plaster down the hair to prevent it from being unruly or untidy. We know the father or disciplinarian who cannot bear to see his sons allowing their hair to grow too long. It is perhaps significant that girls or women (who have no penis) are allowed by society to grow their hair rather longer than men. It is not offensive in them.

In this connection attention should be drawn to the punishment of shearing the hair, spontaneously inflicted by the people of liberated regions in France upon women who were alleged to be 'collaborators'.

The bald patches in the dream which represented an extreme attempt at politeness, a complete castration, remind us of the social convention of being completely bald about the face and chin—of shaving.

Are we in shaving doing the same thing as this patient did in the dream—to please the woman (i.e., to renounce the Oedipus desire for the mother)?

This same patient did have a dream about shaving but I shall not deal with it in *detail* as we wish to get on to other matters.

Briefly the dream was that he was about to be shaved by a particular barber. The barber put the razor across his mouth and slit it. He tasted the blood.

His associations to this barber are that he was a horrible ruffian whom he would avoid at all costs if it came to shaving. He was forced as a boy, in spite of his fears and objections, to have his hair cut by this man.

His other associations are to an occasion on which he was operated upon for hernia. The matron of the nursing home shaved his pubic hair on the morning of the operation. He was frightened at first but subsequently as a result of her 'operations' he had ever since had a strong love attachment to her. We thus see a connection in this dream between shave, operation, love, and assault.

The dream shows the patient in the feminine role being, not shaved, but raped by the father instead. It occurs to us to think of the possible relationship of accidental cuts during shaving to an unconscious desire to make the shaving more thorough-going—to make it in fact not merely a castration but even a rape, thereby perhaps compensating for the castration by experiencing a feminine gratification as the patient did in his dream at the hands of the father. At any rate the cut, like the mutilation, seems to be something in the nature of the shave only more extreme—so extreme as to be resisted and to arouse conflict. In the barber dream the

libidinal wish (for the father image to rape him) is dramatised in the act of being cut, and the ego-resistance, causing
conflict, in the horror. All nightmares are produced by this
conflict.

Our clinical material need not be limited to dreams. One
gets actual symptoms or even whole cases which throw
light upon the subject under discussion.

I am reminded of the female patient at the menopause
who came for treatment on account of a habit of rubbing her
hair in one place. This habit was so persistent that she
rubbed a hole in every cap she wore (she was a housemaid).
The history was significant : the habit began at fifteen years
of age. She had been masturbating. (She had been rubbing
her genitals—she has been rubbing her *hair* ever since.) She
struggled against the impulse to masturbate and suppressed
it. It was then that she went into an orchard and stole apples
(restoration of the castration).[1] While doing so she fancied
that an earwig had crept into her ear. In consequence she
felt an irritation and rubbed her head above the ear. This
rubbing had persisted ever since—a period of thirty years.

We can only think of one source from which such an
absorbing and persistent energy could be derived.

The unconscious mechanisms at work are pretty clear.
The unconscious incestuous phantasy accompanying the
masturbation was repressed on account of strong Oedipus
guilt. It escaped from repression in the form of apple stealing. The incestuous wish with its impregnation corollary
expressed itself in the delusion of the earwig having
penetrated her ear (vagina). Erotic (masturbation) impulses
were expressed (and partly gratified) in the hair rubbing.
The guilt attaching to the whole Oedipus phantasy is easily
detected in the patient's state of mind and in the punishment
which the neurotic habit inflicts upon her ego.

[1] A. S. Neill, who bases his theories entirely upon his ordinary observations of
schoolchildren, affirms that stealing in children is invariably a masturbation
substitute—that it arises as the result of suppression of masturbation.

The symptom is clearly (as are all symptoms) a compromise formation or a condensation of (genital) libido and repression thereof. Its relevance for our purpose is that again it is to the hair (or at least to the region of the hair) that the genital conflict has been displaced.

Dr. Eder describes how a woman who suffered from pronounced castration fear (anxiety hysteria) kept putting off her shingling appointment. At last she kept it but was taken ill with the first cut. He refers to similar experiences in normal people and quotes a hairdresser as saying he is accustomed to his clients failing to keep numerous appointments. A normal woman on the night prior to her appointment for shingling dreamt that her son was drowned in the swimming bath and awoke with intense anxiety.[1]

Ernest Simmel describes the case of his boy aged three and a half who was playfully threatened castration with scissors by the surgeon who had circumcised him. The child, who had stood the operation without alarm, became terrified at the playful threat. A year later he related his visit to the surgeon in great detail but substituted 'haircut' in place of the castration threat. Simmel says the conscious idea of cutting off the hair had taken the place of the unconscious idea of cutting off the penis.[2] (There appeared to be only two references to hair in *The International Journal of Psycho-Analysis*, and both papers are dated 1925, until the publication of my paper in January, 1936.)

From a consideration of the material presented so far we can formulate a theory of our hair activities. In the first case quoted : what binds the patient to his mistress is genital affect. The source of his pleasure in exposing her pubic hair is genital. His pleasure affect is experienced in the dream in pressing the head hair of the red-headed girl. We thus see

[1] M. D. Eder : 'A Note on Shingling.' *International Journal of Psycho-Analysis*, Vol. VI, Part 3.

[2] Ernest Simmel : 'A Screen Memory in Statu Nascendi.' *International Journal of Psycho-Analysis*, Vol. VI, Part 4.

that the genital affect is displaced via the pubic hair to the hair of the head.

In the second case the manifest content of the dream is :

(1) Exceptionally short hair—shorter than the patient ever wears it nowadays. The latent content that gives rise to this is the fact that the patient *feels* castrated.

(2) Manifest content shows the analyst restoring this hair by rubbing it. The latent content is the hope that the analyst will restore not the hair but the penis by his analytical massage.

(3) The white lather is the wish fulfilment. The penis is restored and functions correctly by emission. (I think there is a deeper anal element here also.)

(4) The anxiety attributed in the dream to the mother is the patient's castration anxiety, 'How can I get my penis back ?'

In the third case we see a conflict between exhibitionism and castration manifested in considerable detail by means of the hair. For the sake of the mother, to retain her love, he has it cut more and more until he is reduced to the pitiful plight that brings him to treatment. In real life he feels castrated (popularly designated as 'inferiority feelings') and an object of ridicule. He attempts to cover his castration and at the same time to control, or to lay flat, his erection.

It is all expressed in terms of hair activities. In addition, attention is called to many of the normal dislikes and preferences towards hair. It is the conflict between sexual impulses at the genital level on the one hand, and the repressing forces of the super-ego and ego on the other hand. Can we not see the same conflict being worked out, without ever reaching a solution, in our normal daily hair activities and in the ever-changing fashions in hair ? This is a characteristic of any and every hysterical symptom— namely, that, in some displaced or converted disguise, the

original sexual conflict at the genital level should be fruit-
lessly seeking solution. Every hysterical symptom is
identical in its *source* (namely genital level of sexual conflict),
in its *mechanism* (namely, displacement or conversion), and
in its *synthesis* of libido and repressing force. What then is
there to distinguish the two except the widely adopted
nature of the hair activity? Is it distinguishable from
hysteria only in that it is mass hysteria?

An important element in the manifestation of this hair
hysteria, an element which is not always absent in ordinary
hysterical symptoms, is that the conflict between libido and
repressing force is manifested largely in the form of exhibitionism versus castration anxiety. It is as though the hair
which we display in our clothed social state were the only
phallus permitted us by society—the only phallus we are
permitted to *reveal*. There is the tendency to show how fine
it is, to be proud of it and sue for its approval, alternating
with a fear lest it should not be approved. This fear is
expressed by brushing it flat, by being sure that it is tidy, or
even by hastening to cut it off ourselves, as in shaving, lest
we should suffer still more serious castration at the hands of
society. At least the anxiety is clearly present and is identical
with castration anxiety.

The normal concern or anxiety about the hair becoming
thin or falling out, alopecia, or becoming grey, are displacements of castration anxiety. Similarly, concern regarding its
appearance, its untidiness, or its erectness are castration
anxieties related to exhibitionism. On the other hand, pride
in its appearance, in its prettiness or social acceptability is a
displacement of exhibitionistic satisfaction. The energy is
sufficient in quantity to give rise to all that elaborate organisation of hairdressers and that repetitive daily ritual with its
attendant expense and time-absorption to which I made
reference in the early part of the paper (£30,000,000 a year
on permanent waving alone). As in all hysterical symptoms

the displacement saves a conflict from solution but provides an outlet for its affective tension. Therefore the repetition goes on *ad infinitum*. This is of course, characteristic of activity which has its source in the unconscious, a source which is left unaffected by conscious experience.

# Anthropological Evidence of the Unconscious Significance of Hair

BEFORE proceeding to a deeper analysis of this genital level of the sexual conflict, we may pause for a moment to consider whether the hair-behaviour and legends of antiquity, of primitive peoples, lend confirmation or refutation to the theories hitherto enunciated.

In my opinion anthropological evidence is not absolutely necessary for our purpose. The behaviour of modern communities with regard to their hair is of the same essential nature as that of ancient and barbarous peoples. It should suffice to re-examine this current hair-behaviour in the light of clinical psycho-analytical discovery to detect in it ample confirmation of our theories. An application of these theories to current hair-behaviour is in fact the implicit object of this monograph. Nevertheless, in so far as we have grown so accustomed to this modern hair-behaviour that we have become blind to its irrelevant nature, it may still be useful to review the behaviour of ancient peoples, which by its novelty may reveal that to which habit has blinded us in *our* customs. Also the remarks of anthropologists, who are not psycho-analysts, will occasionally be seen to lend confirmation to theories of which they themselves were unaware.

Amongst the Trobriand Islanders the essential feature of mourning is the complete shaving of the hair of the scalp. This is of interest as being in keeping with the unconscious equation : loss of the loved person=castration=removal of hair. In dreams the removal of a person's hair or beard is a common symbol for castration of that person. In this connection it is well to remember the Red Indian custom of removing the scalp of a fallen enemy and to compare this to the parallel Biblical custom of cutting off his foreskin. The Arabs had a custom of removing his entire genitalia. The death of a loved person or relative is felt by the unconscious to be a castration, and this in the custom of the Trobriand Islanders is dramatised by the shaving of the bereaved (castrated) person's hair.

Towards the end of the last section it was stated that pride in the appearance of the hair, its prettiness or social acceptability is a displacement of exhibitionistic satisfaction. Now we will see how the behaviour of these Islanders confirms this theory. I would draw special attention to Malinowski's remarks (at the end of his description) to the effect that this elaborate behaviour does not weary the savages, as it does the European observer, because *for them it contains a pronounced erotic element*. It is apparent that this erotic element is exhibitionistic, and that the hair display is but a substitute for genital exhibitionism :

'After a long period during which no deaths have occurred so that the people have been able to grow long hair, a display of this highly-valued natural beauty is held. Only men take part in this *kayasa*. They adorn themselves, spread mats on the central place, and, tearing out their hair with the long-pronged Melanesian comb, they sing and display its charm. The women admire and pronounce judgment on the quality and beauty of the hair.'

They then adorn themselves with shell ornaments, and day after day, evening after evening, parade the central place.

'To a European observer the proceedings appear unspeakably monotonous and pointless. The repetition for weeks on end . . . But for the native . . . the whole affair has an intense interest and considerable attraction. In this sex plays a considerable part. For the desire to show off, to produce a personal effect, to achieve "butura" (renown) in its most valued form, that of irresistible charm, contains a pronounced erotic element.'[1]

The anthropological material is so abundant that a classification of it all would present an enormous task. I shall content myself with a few typical excerpts :

Examples of hair being regarded as the *seat of strength* :

'The Australian custom of depositing the hair with the dead is interesting, for it is a common notion that the hair is the seat of strength.'[2]

'Just as Samson's miraculous strength went from him when his hair was shorn, so it is believed that the head chief of the Masai would lose his supernatural powers if his chin were shaved.'[3]

If we enquire further into the mysterious nature of this strength invested in the hair we discover that it is held to have *fertilising* powers :

'If the sacrifice of hair, especially of hair at puberty, is sometimes intended to strengthen the divine beings to whom it is offered by feeding or fertilising them, we can better understand, not only the common practice of offering hair to the shadowy dead, but also the Greek usage of shearing it for rivers, as the Arcadian boys of Phigalia did for the stream that runs in the depths of the tremendous woody glen below the city. For next perhaps to rain and sunshine, nothing in nature so obviously contributes to fertilise a country as its rivers. Again, this view may set in a clearer light the custom of the Delian youths and maidens who offered their hair on the maidens' tomb under the olive tree. For at Delos as at Delphi one of Apollo's many functions was to make crops grow and to fill the husbandman's barn.'[4]

[1]Bronislaw Malinowski : *The Sexual Life of Savages*, page 216.
[2]Frazer : *The Golden Bough*, Book I, Vol. I, page 102.
[3]Ibid, Book I, Vol. I, page 344.
[4]Ibid, Book I, Vol. I, page 31.

Further evidence of the genital value of the strength resident in hair may be found in the ceremony of hair cutting as a purification :

'This view is borne out by a practice observed by some Australians of burning off part of a woman's hair after childbirth, as well as burning every vessel which has been used by her during her seclusion;'[1]

and the taboo on the hair-cutting of the virgin before defloration :

'When a girl reaches puberty, the Wafiomi of Eastern Africa hold a festival, at which they make a noise with a peculiar kind of rattle. After that the girl remains for a year in a large common hut, but where she occupies a special compartment screened off from the men's quarters. She *may not cut her hair* or touch food, but is fed by other women. At night however she quits the hut and dances with the young men.'[2]

Preservation of virginity is apparently equated here with preservation of hair. In conformity with this we find innumerable examples of the sacrifice of hair being equated with the surrender of the genitals.

'Novices had their hair cut at initiation. In Fiji the novices were shaved and their beards, if they had any, were carefully eradicated.'[3]

In the hair-behaviour of savages we may trace the working out of the genital level of sexual conflict in even greater detail : There are for instance innumerable examples of placating the rival parent by a symbolic genital surrender *in the form of hair.*

'The custom observed by Troezenian girls of offering tresses of their hair to Hippolytus before their wedding brings him into relation with marriage, which at first sight seems out of keeping with his reputation as a

[1]Frazer : *The Golden Bough*, Book III, page 284.
[2]Ibid, Book X, Vol. I, page 28.
[3]Ibid, Book XI, Vol. II, page 245.

confirmed bachelor. According to Lucian, youths as well as maidens at Troezen were forbidden to wed till they had shorn their hair in honour of Hippolytus, and we gather from the context that it was their first beard which the young men thus polled. *However we may explain it,* a custom of this sort appears to have prevailed widely in Greece and in the East. Plutarch tells us that formerly it was the wont of boys at puberty to go to Delphi and offer of their hair to Apollo ; Theseus, father of Hippolytus, complied with the custom which lasted down into historical times. Argive maidens grown to womanhood dedicated their tresses to Athena before marriage. On the same occasion Megarian girls poured libations and laid clippings of their hair on the tomb of the maiden Iphinoe.

'At the entrance to the temple of Artemis in Delos the grave of two maidens was shown under an olive tree. It is said that long ago they had come as pilgrims from a far northern land with offerings to Apollo and dying in the sacred isle were buried there. The Delian virgins before marriage used to cut off a lock of their hair, wind it on a spindle and lay it on the maidens' grave. The young men did the same, except that they twisted the down of their first beard round a wisp of grass or a green shoot. In some places it was Artemis who received the offering of a maiden's hair before marriage. At Panamara in Caria men dedicated locks of their hair in the temple of Zeus. The locks were enclosed in little stone boxes, some of them fitted with a marble lid or shutter, and the name of the dedicator was engraved on a square sinking in the stone, together with the name of the priest for the time being. Many of these inscribed boxes have been found of late years on the spot. None of them bear the names of women ; some of them are inscribed with the name of a father and his sons. All the dedications are to Zeus alone, though Hera was also worshipped with him at Panamara.

At Hierapolis on the Euphrates, girls offered of their tresses and youths of their beards to the great Syrian goddess, and left shorn hair in caskets of gold and silver inscribed with their names, and nailed to the wall of the temple. The custom of dedicating the first beard seems to have been common at Rome under the Empire. Thus Nero consecrated his first beard in a golden box studded with costly pearls on the Capitol.'[1]

If any should doubt the unconscious genital symbolism of these hair offerings he may read a little further :

'In the sanctuary of the great Phoenecian goddess Astarte at Byblus the practice was different. Here, at the annual mourning for the dead Adonis, the women had to shave their heads, and such of them as refused to do so were bound to prostitute themselves to strangers and to sacrifice to the goddess with the wages of their shame. Though Lucian, who mentions the custom, does not say so, there are grounds for thinking that the women in question were generally women of whom this act of devotion was required as a preliminary to marriage. *In any case it is clear that the goddess accepted the sacrifice of chastity as a substitute for the sacrifice of hair.*'[2] (The italics are mine.)

To continue the quotation :

'*Why ? By many people, as we shall afterwards see, the hair is regarded as in a special sense the seat of strength*; and at puberty it might well be thought it contained a double portion of vital energy, since at that season it is the outward sign and manifestation of the newly-acquired power of reproducing the species. *For that reason, we may suppose, the beard rather than the hair of the head is offered by the male on this occasion.* Thus the substitution permitted at *Byblus* becomes intelligible ; the women gave of their

[1]Frazer : *The Golden Bough*, Book I, Vol. I, page 28, etc.
[2]Ibid, Book I, Vol. I, page 28, etc.

fecundity to the goddess, whether they offered their hair
or their chastity.'

Perhaps we can answer his further enquiry :

'But why, it may be asked should they make such an
offering to Astarte, who was herself the great goddess of
love and fertility ? What need had she to receive fecundity
from her worshippers ? Was it not rather for her to
bestow it on them ? Thus put, the question overlooks an
important side of polytheism, perhaps we may say of
ancient religion in general. The gods stood as much in
need of their worshippers as the worshippers in need of
them. The benefits conferred were mutual. If the gods
made the earth to bring forth abundantly, the flocks and
herds to teem, and the human race to multiply, they
expected that a portion of their bounty should be returned
to them in the shape of tithe or tribute. On this tithe,
indeed, they subsisted, and without it they would starve.
Their divine bellies had to be filled, and their divine
reproductive energies to be recruited ; hence the men had
to give of their meat and drink to them, and to sacrifice
for their benefit what is most *manly in men and womanly in
woman*. Sacrifices of the latter kind have too often been
overlooked or misunderstood by the historians of
religion. Other examples of them will meet us in the
course of our enquiry. At the same time it may well be that
the women who offered their hair to Astarte hoped to
benefit through the sympathetic connection which they
thus established between themselves and the goddess ;
they may in fact have expected to fecundate themselves
by contact with the divine source of fecundity. It is
probable that a similar motive underlay the sacrifice of
chastity as well as the sacrifice of hair.'

We see here that little distinction is made between the
sacrifice of the genitals and the sacrifice of hair. The two are

clearly identified in these practices. Hair is here a symbol of the genital. While allowing Frazer's explanation as far as it goes we may add that the essence of initiation is the placating of the rival parent by a symbolical sacrifice of the genital to him or her, and surely Astarte, the goddess of fertility, was such a parent figure.

I have drawn attention to the exhibitionistic convenience of hair as a phallic symbol. Examples of the connection of hair with the exhibitionism of genital potency are not lacking in the anthropological literature :

> 'In Uganda a father of twins does not have his hair cut for a time . . . or to distinguish him from the common herd his hair is cut in a special way and he wears little bells at his ankles which tinkle as he walks . . . he may neither dress his hair nor cut his finger nails.'[1]

Long hair as a symbol of royalty :

> 'The Caesars, the most illustrious family of the Julian house, took their name from their long hair (Caesaries), which was probably in those early days as it was amongst the Franks long afterwards, a symbol of royalty.'[2]

A brief review of some other literature on the subject of hair may be of value :

Havelock Ellis[3] regards hair as perhaps the most common and most important *fetish* and as a possible link of transition between the bodily origin of fetishism and its more remote objects such as animals and stuffs.[4] In connection with fetishism Krafft-Ebing remarks that the senses of touch, smell and hearing, as well as sight, seem to enter into the attraction exerted by hair.

The verses of Lovelace 'To Althea from Prison' are

[1]Frazer : *The Golden Bough*, Book II, Vol. II, page 102.
[2]Ibid, Book II, Vol. II, page 179.
[3]Havelock Ellis : *Studies in the Psychology of Sex*, Vol. V, page 74.
[4]Psycho-analysis has shown us that a fetish is always (*a*) a phallic symbol, (*b*) a castrated phallus and (*c*) the mother's phallus.

interesting as selecting the hair and the eyes for special fetishtic attention :

'When I lie tangled in her hair
And fettered to her eye,
The birds that wanton in the air
Know no such liberty.'

Note the use of the word 'wanton' in connection with the phallic symbol of 'Birds'. The phantasy is unconsciously a symbolic presentation of coitus, and seen in the light of this interpretation it is obvious that, under the circumstances described by the poet, the 'bird' (sexuality) would 'wanton' in a new-found liberty.

Havelock Ellis declares that hair is sexually the most generally noted part of the feminine body after the eyes,[1] and this apparently for good reasons for he establishes a connection between the qualities of the hair and the potency or sexual virility of the individual. Thus :

'Of all physical traits vigour of the hairy system has most frequently perhaps been regarded as the index of vigorous sexuality. In this matter modern medical observations are at one with popular belief and ancient physiognomical assertions. The negative test of castration and the positive test of puberty point in the same direction.

'It is at puberty that all the hair on the body except that on the head, begins to develop ; indeed, the very word "puberty" has reference to this growth as the most obvious sign of the whole process. *When castration takes place at an early age all this development of pubescent hair is arrested.* When the primary sexual organs are undeveloped the sexual hair is also undeveloped, as in a case recorded by Plant, of a girl with rudimentary uterus and ovaries who had little or no axillary and pubic hair although the hair of the head was long and strong.'[2]

[1]Havelock Ellis : *Studies in the Psychology of Sex*, Vol. V, page 75.
[2]Ibid, Vol. V, page 194.

Della Porta, the greatest of the physiognomists, said that the thickness of the hair in women meant wantonness.

Venette, in his Génération de l'Homme, remarked that men who have much hair on the body are most amorous.

At a more recent period Roubaud has said that pubic hair in its quantity, colour and curliness is an index of genital energy. A poor pilous system, on the other hand, Roubaud regarded as a probable though not an irrefragible proof of sexual frigidity in women.

'In the cold woman the pilous system is remarkable for the langour of its vitality ; the hairs are fair, delicate, scarce and smooth, while in ardent natures there are little curly tufts about the temples.'[1]

Martineau declared that :

'The more developed the genital organs the more abundant the hair covering them ; abundance of hair appears to be in relation to the perfect development of the organs.'[2]

Tardieu described the typically erotic woman as very hairy.

After referring to these and other matters Havelock Ellis goes on to say :

'It is a very ancient and popular belief that if a hairy man is not sensual he is strong.

'It may be doubted whether there is any exact parallelism between muscular strength and hairiness, for strength is largely a matter of training, but there can be no doubt that hairiness really tends to be associated with a generally vigorous development of the body.'[3]

The psycho-analyst may pause to consider whether both the hairiness and the physical development may not be due to a libidinisation of the body.

[1] *Traité de l'Impuissance*, pp. 124, 523.
[2] *Leçons sur les Déformations Vulvaires*, p. 40.
[3] Havelock Ellis : *Studies in the Psychology of Sex*, Vol. V, p. 196.

Havelock Ellis again :

'We thus see that it is quite justifiable to admit a type of person who possesses a more than average aptitude for detumescence. Such persons are more likely to be short than tall ; they will show a full development of secondary sexual characters ; the voice will tend to be deep and the eyes bright ; the glandular activity of the skin will probably be marked ; the lips everted ; there is a tendency to a more than average degree of pigmentation, and there is frequently an abnormal prevalence of hair on some parts of the body.'[1]

(We are warned however that there are exceptions to this rule, e.g., degeneration of the ovaries in women is commonly accompanied by some hairy growth about the face.)

Róheim seems to push the matter further and to see in the *down*-ceremonies of the Arunda peoples a mere later edition of what nature performs with pro-chemical and physical agents, instead of down and artificial decorations, in the case of animals :

'The males of the higher mammals perform an Itata (a ceremonial of hetero-sexual licence) in the rutting season, before they fecundate their females. They do not put on a kutara (peaked hat made of bushes), but they develop manes, antlers or other secondary sexual characters.'[2]

If the statements of these observers are correct it would seem that nature has biologically or physically established a close connection between libidinal or sexual energy and a growth of hair. Such a connection would be a parallel in the physical world to that to which I am drawing attention in the mental world, namely, that affects associated with hair on a conscious plane correspond to affects associated with repressed libido on an unconscious plane.

[1]Havelock Ellis : *Studies in the Psychology of Sex*, Vol. V, p. 197.
[2]Róheim : *International Journal of Psycho-Analysis*, Vol. XIII, Parts 1 and 2, p. 68.

If these observers are mistaken, if there is nothing in reality corresponding to their 'observations', one would then ask whence they obtained their erroneous views. The only possible answer would be from their own (presumably normal) minds. Such an answer will serve our purpose equally well, for it will establish that such a connection (between hair and libido) exists in the minds of normal men, and it is this mental association, the unconscious significance of hair, with which we are here concerned.

# Evidence from Folklore and Legend of the Unconscious Significance of Hair

NOT less ample than the evidence to be found in anthropology, nor less confirmatory of the theories enunciated in this paper, is the evidence available from folk-lore, legend and literary reference.

The common superstition that horse-hairs falling into water grow into eels and water-snakes[1] links the individual hair with one of the commonest of genital symbols, and leads us to the legend of the Gorgon's head, which was covered with living snakes in the place of hair, its aspect being so terrible that any mortal beholder was turned to stone. It would indeed seem to represent the parent's genitals, which must not, under threat of direct penalties, be looked at by the offspring. (Cf. the strict Jewish prohibition against beholding the nakedness of the parent.)[2]

The benevolent father-figure has a beard that may be viewed without danger. It is a great white beard. This is seen in the folk-conception of the benevolent magician, e.g., Merlin, in pictorial representations of God the Father, and in the comparatively modern Santa Claus. The irresponsible id-figure, however, must not have white hair : 'How ill white hairs become a fool and jester.'[3]

The bad father-figure, on the other hand, has a terrifying beard, like Blue-beard in the story, who punishes the inquisitive girl when she succeeds in finding out the nature of the brutal assault he commits against his wife when he enters into the little room whose floor he has caused to flow with blood.[4]

[1] A. R. Wright : *Folklore*.
[2] Leviticus XX, 11.
[3] Shakespeare : *Henry V*, v. 3.
[4] Perrault : *Contes de la Mère L'Oie*

There would seem to be a quality of magic potency about the long beard, and even long hair, although proverbs English, French and Russian all equate 'Long hair and little wit.' Such beard and hair are the traditional attribute of the magician, the prophet and the poet. Gray's description of the Bard :

> 'Loose his beard and hoary hair
> Streamed like a meteor to the troubled air'[1]

may serve as typical, and may be compared with the warning against one who has 'drunk the milk of Paradise' :

> 'Beware ! Beware !
> His flashing eyes, his floating hair.'[2]

In dreams also feelings of magical potency are commonly accompanied by the concept of floating through the air. Analysis reveals that they have their origin in eroticism, suggesting that the hair symbolism and magical concepts associated with it are their sublimated equivalents.

In woman, fair hair, perhaps as being less nearly related to the pubic hair, is taken as symbolical of purity, as in Faust's Gretchen. Nevertheless, perhaps the strongest evidence of the inevitability of this reaction to fair hair is the frequency of warnings that it is no true index : e.g. the proverb : 'All are not maidens that wear fair hair'[3] and Longfellow's :

> 'Often treachery lies
> Underneath the fairest hair.'[4]

Even Goethe himself writes :

> 'Beware of her fair hair for she excels
> All women in the magic of her locks ;
> And when she winds them round a young man's neck
> She will not ever let him free again.'[5]

[1] Thomas Gray : *The Bard*
[2] Coleridge : *Kubla Khan*
[3] John Ray : *Compleat Collection of English Proverbs*, 1670
[4] Longfellow : *Saga of King Olaf*
[5] Goethe : *Faust* (Shelley's Translation)

It would seem that the mermaidens who lure men to their doom, profit, like the Lorelei, by this unreasonable confidence which fair hair inspires. For this confidence is a very real thing, and, despite all warnings, the princess in the fairy story always has golden hair.

One such golden-haired princess of legend provides us with an outstanding example of the permissible nature of hair-exhibitionism, and a hint that the potent woman may overcome inhibitions that cause impotence in the man. She is incarcerated at the top of a tower, and her lover cannot reach her. However, she overcomes her lover's powerlessness (i.e. impotence) by displaying her hair at its full length, thus providing him with a ladder by means of which he may enter into her narrow cell.

Perrault's *Riquet à la Houppe* has as its hero a youth who, though born a prince, was so ugly and so repulsive to behold that at first it was doubted whether he were of human shape. Nevertheless he was exceedingly clever. His principal physical characteristic was the little tuft of hair from which he took his name. The heroine is a princess of unequalled beauty, but of absolute lack of intelligence. She cannot even place four porcelain vessels on the mantelshelf without breaking one, nor drink a glass of water without spilling half of it upon herself.

Riquet à la Houppe meets her, and as a result she comes forth endowed with mental gifts the equal of his own. It is to be noted that this meeting, which transformed the stupid (therefore innocent) maiden into a witty woman, took place in a wood.[1]

Attention may here be drawn to a remedy of folk medicine, common, at least until recent years, in London. The eating of a cooked mouse was prescribed as a cure for incontinence of urine.[2] Is it not permissible to draw a parallel

[1] Perrault: *Contes de la Mère L'Oie*
[2] A. R. Wright: *Folklore*

between the cure of the princess who spilt water, by her meeting a repulsive little hairy man in a wood, and the cure of the child who wets his bed by the incorporation of a repulsive little hairy animal, or, leaving the symbolism of hair, to extend the metaphor to its more general significance : the cure of innocence and the ills thereof and the acquisition of maturity and its major troubles by eating the forbidden apple of knowledge, a less phallic and more feminine symbol of sexuality.

Apart from fairness, the quality of curliness in hair is traditionally important in the love object. This applies to the male as much as to the female. Charis, asked by Ben Jonson to 'describe her man' demands :

> 'crisped hair
> Cast in a thousand snares and rings
> For Love's fingers and his wings.'

As to his beard :
> 'His lip should kissing teach
> Till he cherished too much beard
> And made Love or me afeard.'[1]

This is clearly a compromise-formation harmonising the desire for and fear of the genitals.

The hair as a part of the body, and as a symbol of the most vital part of the body, is to the folk-mind an index and a representative of life itself. Hair burning brightly when cast into the fire is an indication of long life.

Apollo's lute, his most characteristic attribute, was strung with his own hair,[2] and, in the Scottish Ballad of the 'Twa Sisters of Binnorie', when the harp made from her breast-bone is strung with her own hair it tells the murdered sister's story, revealing that the other sister had precipitated her into the mill-dam.

[1]Ben Jonson : *Charis Describes Her Man*
[2]Shakespeare : *Romeo and Juliet*, iv. 3.

In two poems John Donne, using the same symbol, makes use of hair as the vital surrogate of the living person :

'Whoever comes to shroud me, do not harm
    Nor question much,
That subtle wreath of hair, which crowns my arm ;
The mystery, the sign you must not touch ;
    For 'tis my outward soul,
Viceroy to that, which unto heaven being gone
    Will leave this to control
And keep these limbs, her provinces, from dissolution.'[1]

In our second example the sexual significance of the wreath of hair is even more apparent :

'When my grave is broken up again
Some second guest to entertain,
    —For graves have learn'd that woman-head,
To be to more than one a bed—
    And he that digs it, spies
A bracelet of bright hair about the bone,
    Will not he let us alone,
And think that there a loving couple lies,
Who thought that this device might be some way
To make their souls at the last busy day
Meet at this grave, and make a little stay ?'[2]

The very title of Pope's mock-epic, 'The Rape of the Lock', is an example of the same underlying idea, which is equally evident in the superstition common amongst dressmakers that 'it is a sign of the worker's own wedding coming soon if she accidentally sews one of her own hairs into a garment of a trousseau.'[3]

In 1914 it was reported in the *Crediton Chronicle* that a man on his way to have a tooth drawn was told by a friend not to go but to adopt the following ritual :

[1] John Donne : *The Funeral*
[2] John Donne : *The Relic*
[3] A. R. Wright : *Folklore*

"to put his arms round a young ash-tree, make a slit in the bark where his fingers met, and then pull out some hair from the back of his head and put it in the slit.'[1]

In keeping with that of an abundance of dream material, the interpretation would seem to be that the aching tooth is equal to the uncomfortable tumid penis, which can be dealt with in two ways, by satisfaction or by castration (i.e. extraction). The method chosen makes doubly sure by adopting both measures, the hair being pulled out but being successful in attaining intromission into the slit made in the virgin tree.

This combination of sexual activity with castration can in the same way be perceived in the biblical story of Absalom, the rebellious son, who penetrates into a forest only to be caught by his luxuriant hair in a tree and left hanging there to be put to death by the darts of his father's men.[2] A pretty little presentation of the Oedipus castration phantasy !

The disgust which hair seems often to incite when detached from the body may, at least in part, be held to derive from anal associations. Such associations may account for the belief that it is unlucky to keep one's own hair combings,[3] and for the use to which in the Tyrol witches are supposed to put cut or combed-out hair to make hailstones and thunder storms.[4] But see the following two sections in which this pre-genital significance of hair is more fully revealed.

[1]A. R. Wright : *Folklore*
[2]II Samuel, Chapter XVIII
[3]A. R. Wright : *Folklore*
[4]Frazer : *The Golden Bough*, Book III, p. 271

# Can the Unconscious Significance of Hair be traced to a Pre-genital Level?

IN tracing man's hair activity to a genital level I have evidently revealed nothing very startling to the anthropologist and still less to the psycho-analyst. The question now arises as to whether we can go further than this. I think we can, and I shall refer to some further clinical material which carries the matter to a level earlier than the genital.

I think this material throws additional light upon the perversion of exhibitionism as well as upon a very early source of hair exhibitionism. I do not think that the theory to which this brings us appears in the literature. Moreover, with one exception, nobody has ever drawn attention to this particular unconscious significance of hair. The notable exception is Dr. Ernest Jones who makes a passing reference to it :

'Hair itself has several sexual meanings, being indeed biologically a secondary sexual characteristic. *One that I do not remember having been pointed out but which I have several times found during psycho-analysis, is an association with faeces.*

' . . . It was a general superstition in the Middle Ages that horse's hair, laid in manure water, turned into poisonous snakes (cf. Medusa's snake-hair).'[1]

As I have said it is obvious from the material produced that there is an important exhibitionistic element in normal hair activity (note the average girl's patting and tidying of her hair even in the face of urgent contingencies), therefore

[1]Ernest Jones : *On the Nightmare*, p. 299. Ernest Jones refers also to Shakespeare's *Antony and Cleopatra*, Act I, Sc. 2.

it is perhaps not surprising that interesting material should come from a patient who has strong exhibitionistic tendencies.

The dream which this patient produced was as follows :

'I put sand or grit upon my face preparatory to shaving, and was about to go into the street to shave. It occurred to me that I should have used a soap lather first and put on this sand afterwards. It was unsatisfactory and I felt some anxiety, but I was too hurried to alter it. I started shaving hurriedly in the street. The sand blunted or rather made jagged the razor edge ; and finally I cut my chin on one side. The blood welled out and kept on bleeding profusely.'

The association to the sand is :

'Brown muddy sand'—and finally : 'Excrement.'

This leads to a memory of infantile exhibition of his bottom. There is a latent content of exhibitionism in :

(1) Appearing in the street for the performance.
(2) In exposing this besmirched chin or face (the dirty anus).
(3) In the public operations with the razor.

Anxiety (a usual accompaniment of exhibitionism) is manifested (1) as such, (2) in the hesitation, and (3) in the hurry. Finally the latent content, *castration*, is manifested in (1) the jagging of the razor blade (his razor blade, his penis), (2) in the removal of the 'sand' or 'excrement,' (3) in the removal of the hair, and (4) finally, in the cutting of the chin. He knew it must end in such an accident.

The persistent welling forth of the blood is associatively connected with menstruation. Thus is phallic-anal guilt expiated by shaving, cutting, or mutilation. *Its relation to exhibitionism is this : It is all very well to have phallic-anal pleasure provided the parents do not see it. The test, exhibitionism, lies here. Will they cut it off or shall we do so first and be safe ?*

In this connection with the anxiety, he felt that if he had first shaved properly indoors, then he could have done this (gone out with the earth on his face) with comparative impunity . . . And don't we all feel the same about our morning operation of shaving? We have only to test it to see how uncomfortable and guilty we feel in public if we forgo our morning shave. Must we be castrated to be safe with our fellow men? Must we be *clean*—free from anal guilt?

This same patient at a later stage of his analysis produces a dream in which a king and queen (parent figures—or projections of super-ego) have become homely persons who prepare and serve dinner to their friends in their kitchen.

His association to the queen is to an attractive but dirty servant girl. He felt sure that she had venereal disease, but he said she was so attractive *that her venereal disease* became attractive and, in phantasy he would willingly share it with her. Anything she had would be lovely—even dirt—*her* dirt.

In short his dream means that the parents are faeces also, but *nice* faeces. His associations continue:

'If I could get to a stage where I didn't *mind* having a dirty anus, if I could feel quite at ease with a dirty anus in spite of its being known and visible, *then* I would have no anxiety about appearing and being seen in public. I would not have to tidy my hair when I was to appear in public. I would not mind if my hair were out of place or untidy.'

I think here we have some revelation of the significance of the constant tidying and fussing about hair that is so frequently seen, particularly in women (who carry a mirror for the purpose). It is an anxiety symptom that has obsessional characters. Its source is anxiety lest the guilt (faeces) should be seen. The tidying is shown as a prelude to appearance in public—for guilt has its source in parental or public condemnation.

There is a little difference here in the hair-behaviour of men and women. Whereas men do their hair-tidying in private or in secret, women have nowadays grown so bold as to do it flagrantly in public. It seems likely that the anxiety (exhibitionistic anxiety—phallic or anal) is greater in men—they must not be seen even attending to it. The modern woman on the other hand, in so far as she attends to it, reveals anxiety or guilt feelings, but in so far as she does this in *public* she reveals an element of defiance[1] which is probably the result of some lessening of the degree of anxiety since Victorian days.

The important point I wish to make from this last clinical material is that our concern over hair can have a pre-genital, namely, an anal source. The bias in favour of *tidiness* and *orderliness*, *cleanliness*, and even *scent*, makes this revelation the more credible.

An interesting point, but one not wholly relevant to our subject is that this clinical material reveals that the perversion of exhibitionism also has a source earlier than the genital, namely, an anal source. The exhibitionist seems to have been concerned not only as to whether the mother would approve or castrate his phallus, but, *earlier than this*, as to whether she would approve or condemn his faeces—whether he could be loved in spite of a dirty anus—or rather because of it. *He is suing for his mother's approval and appreciation of what he himself (as a baby) loves and appreciates so much, namely, his faeces, his anal erotism.*

In case the problem of the symbolism of hair may appear to be more simple than it really is I shall give another extract from clinical material.

This example has the advantage, not only of showing the complexity of the displacement, but also of introducing anal elements. It is from the same patient whom I mentioned before as having his sexual life limited to homosexual

[1] J. C. Flugel: *The Psychology of Clothes*, p. 189

phantasy. The central feature of this is usually a phantasy of caning, or being caned by, the young male love-object.

His erotic activities have for a long time included considerable interest in his special love-object's hair. Speaking of this interest during a session he says :

'I wondered if it were some transformation of the pubic hair on to his head. His head hair is soft and smooth and long. His pubic hair would not have any interest for me. It is too rough and short and wiry. I should dislike his pubic hair because of some reference to the anus. I'd rather it (his bottom) were smooth and hairless and that he had no hair on his legs or thighs. Also a moustache would spoil him as a love-object. All this reminds me of myself : At about the time that I was caned I did not have any hair. My thighs, bottom, etc., were smooth and hairless as I was only a boy. Yet if the hair on his *head* is not uncut (that is to say unless it is longish) it is not attractive.

'In a lavatory I saw a bad drawing of a woman's genitals. The would-be artist had given her too much hair. My thoughts went on to wondering if this hair on Mr. A's head is a displacement of the hair on the mother's genitals . . .

'In my phantasy of embracing Mr. A. I'd be inclined to press my nose against his hair, because the smell of his hair would give me some satisfaction, like smelling his hat. I get as near as possible to doing this in real life when I am leaning over him. I can remember it giving me a slight erection . . . The smell of his hair is all I get. I like the smell of my own hair or hat. I like all my own smells—armpit, sweat, wind, or at the lavatory. The only smells that interest me are my own smells and those of a love-object. I would not contradict a statement that my mother's smells would at some early age have been equally thrilling to me. I have to be content with smells given off by Mr. A. because I cannot touch his bottom.'

What is at first sight puzzling here is the fact that the patient likes the hair on the head as an erotic stimulus, but dislikes the idea of hair about the genitals or anus.

May the key to the situation be (as one of his associations suggests) a displacement of the early *positive element* of interest in his mother's pubic hair (originally genital or anal interest) on to head-hair with a concomitant repression (originally reaction formation against anus and genital) of genital (or anal) hair ?[1] In this way, as with symptom-formation, a conflict is abreacted by a cathexis in symbolical or displaced form of its opposing elements.

What is clearer is that a hairless condition of the sexual regions corresponds to the period of fixation in connection with his own caning experiences.

We thus see that if a displacement from the genitals (and anus) to the head hair does take place it does not necessarily seem to be by way of the intermediate link of pubic hair.

The extract is quoted not merely for the sake of this qualifying problem, but also for the fact that the hair interest here shows considerable reference to anal matters.

It starts with the erotic influence of the *smell* of the love-object's hair and proceeds with associations leading to anal smells, and to other similarly attractive experiences.

In addition to this we must remember that this patient's principal erotic interest is in (young men's) *bottoms*. This is, of course, the positive aspect of his anal erotism.

Amongst the negative (repressive) aspects we may note that he goes through life wearing an expression of disgust; as I have heard it put, 'As though he had a bad smell under his nose.'

The following excerpt from an analytical session may throw further light upon the part hair symbolism can play in the fundamental conflict of all neuroses, namely, the

[1] Advertisements such as that for Veet and other depilatories seem to draw a facile distinction between 'Hair' and '*Ugly hair*'.

conflict between Id and Super-ego[1] within the Oedipus situation, and prior to its arrival at genital organisation.

A patient of mine suffering from a deep-seated inferiority complex with compensatory pride in his intellectual achievements, a patient who wears a monocle and speaks in a high-pitched voice, told me that on entering a club the previous evening he was greeted by a robust acquaintance with a mocking imitation of himself in a high falsetto. This hurt his pride considerably. But another man, newly-introduced to him, was greatly impressed by his manifest 'superiority' and revealed his respect by calling him 'Sir' and raising his hat on my patient's departure. For some reason he associated these incidents with the dream he had that night of which he could remember only the following solitary fragment:

Dream: He was going to an important meeting such as a conference or perhaps even a Royal Garden Party. But the main thing in the dream was that he was going through terrible agonies trying to make a tuft of his hair lie down flat. He could not make it lie down; it would stand up—to his intense discomfort. Thus he had to go to the meeting with this humiliating disadvantage. (End of dream).

In association he said: 'This tuft of hair standing up did not mean that I was more potent so much as it meant that I was unacceptable. My association of thought in trying to make this hair lie down is to try and make the erection lie down. Not a thing that anyone would find acceptable, not a nice erection, but something that was most definitely socially reprehensible *as though one had a faecal penis*. Far from it being any fun to have such a thing, it was a castration in itself. Even as a child one would not feel a grand fellow at having messed one's trousers, no matter what pleasure you

---

[1] Modern psycho-analytical theory would say the conflict is between Id and Ego *plus* Super-ego. But this is a technical refinement.

would assume the id experienced in the relief. It would ostracise one socially ; castrate one. It is dreadfully like my inferiority complex. I can see now what my high-pitched voice is. It is repudiating the penis and at the same time attempting to put on a better one, a genital one, one of which the parents will approve. But the reason that the penis cannot be approved is because it is definitely dirty, repulsive, made of faeces. I have to be rid of it to be potent, or socially potent, so I go to the other extreme and affect a high-pitched voice ; or, as that man in the club seemed to suggest, a highfalutin voice, to show that I am *clean* (i.e. free from faeces) and not only acceptable but socially better. I am trying to achieve a sort of social potency in lieu of the dirty thing which I have, in keeping with society, repudiated. It is because the penis is faecal that it must be cleared away. It was too strong meat, too definitely id. I must go to the other extreme ; get rid of it and replace it by its opposites, its opposites being my high-pitched voice, my monocle and my intellectual achievements—not to speak of my ultra cleanliness. These are a sort of social potency which I am trying to bolster up in lieu of my faecal-penis-id castration.'

The relevance of this excerpt is that it shows the utilisation of the tuft of hair as a faeces-penis symbol, and the difficulty in manipulating it as a symbol for these basic conflicts. It leads us to a better realisation of the significance of our own hair activities as an expression of similar conflicting id and super-ego interests.

There is one other little bit of clinical material that I would like to quote as it seems to confirm the theories so far propounded. It also has the advantage of introducing a deeper problem : namely, the question of the dependence of the body upon its mental equivalent in the unconscious. I quote (verbatim) from the associations of a severe obsessional case.

He says

'The thought comes to toss myself off in B . . . (the firm he works for). I would faint instead. My parents would see that I was all penis and s—. The penis is only s— and piss and my parents would see it.'

A. 'Would that matter ?'

P. 'It would matter at B . . ., or in front of a client.'

A. 'But you were speaking of infancy.'

P. 'Yes, I felt it as a baby. If this penis does break through the skin the next time my mother looks at me she'd see just the top of a penis—my head would just have the shape of the top of a penis.'

A. 'Would that matter ?'

P. 'It would matter because the penis had beaten me. Because it would be like relinquishing life. That is, my penis would take up the whole room that was me. It would matter if you were pushed off an island in the middle of the sea. I felt I became all penis except the top of my brain. All the rest of me was penis and I kept wondering why my mother did not notice it.

'I had a dream last night :

'I looked at the back of a man—a musical comedy actor—and noticed the back of his head, and I saw the hair was going thin in streaks. He had not got alopecia but thin strands of hair and baldness. I thought "What a pity" and then I *worried* as though it were my hair and it was me.'

He continues : 'My worry about this baldness is like being afraid that the penis would come out and show itself. Now and again when I looked at my hair I thought, "Oh ! good Lord ! now it will go again and I will be bald and lose my job !" (This patient had alopecia a few years ago.)

'It is like this feeling that my mind would open and reveal everything. Sometimes I feel I have not any

47

eyebrows, and this baldness . . . this baldness . . . is like being naked and walking about naked with the penis cut off to the hilt and there was nothing . . . it was cut off —flush with the body. In public I would feel unimportant as if I had no penis.'

A. 'This tall and handsome musical comedy actor ?'

P. 'Perhaps *he was my penis*, and that is why I could see him and was worried about his hair.[1] What I was *really* worried about was the length of my penis that was cut off.

'Then I think of those terrible things before I had my penis cut off—before the nurse's masturbation when I wanted to go inside my mother. I wondered if I then decided to cut off my penis. I did not want to do it and yet I felt it was either the penis or me.'

And again from another session :

'When I sat in your chair my thought was how much more guilty I'd have felt if I'd had on the soiled shirt that I wore yesterday. It's all to do with excrement. Now I can see that the "black spot" that worried me as a baby is a great s— hole . . . and this little penis that I wanted to put in my mother was *a pipe leading out from all this muck*. It wasn't an innocent white little clean thing. The arse-hole may have at some time given me the *same pleasure-feeling* as the penis-feeling . . . I mixed up the penis and the arse.

'If I put this penis in my mother and came (orgasm) it would be like letting out a lot of s— . . . filling her with s— . . . not the right way to treat her . . . because it would *kill* her.'

[1] It is my experience that, whenever a figure that appears in a dream is conspicuous for his *hair*, that figure is a genital symbol. In this dream he is seen to be a phallic symbol (as is usual) ; in the dream first quoted (the red-headed girl) the figure was a female genital. Surely this fact, observed in dream-analysis, throws some light on the popular interest in, the focusing of emotional concern upon, the qualities of a person's hair. (Even the unanalysed reader *may* be able to experience the truth of this statement by direct insight.)

It seems from this patient's associations that his obsessional worries about his hair and his alopecia are a manifestation or symptom of the repressed conflict between genital-anal libido and ego. We can detect, hiding behind the phallic anxiety, a still deeper and more important conflict at the anal level. He even says : 'My penis is only s—.' Of course, it was the aggression ('it would kill her') concealed behind the symbolism of faeces which was so dangerous (projected aggression)—and that is why faecal matter is normally hated so much.[1]

I think this material contains a strong suggestion that the normal concern over hair and the anxiety which is so commonly met with amongst normal persons over losing their hair are also manifestations of an obsessional nature having similar unconscious sources. They are only distinguishable from the symptoms of this patient in the matter of their degree rather than of their nature or quality.

A problem that this case raises is that of the relationship of his actual physical alopecia to a content of his unconscious. It is suggestive that the text-books on alopecia place 'worry' as an important aetiological factor. The general term 'worry' as used in these text-books could be more explicitly defined in the terms of the conflict (id [libido and aggression] versus ego) revealed in such a case as this. It seems that the unconscious conflict is whether to be all penis-faeces and no ego, or all ego and no penis-faeces, while the actual physical

[1]During the First World War (1914-18) our soldiers used to refer to the enemy's artillery bombardment as the throwing of 's—' about ; e.g., 'They ain't half throwing some s— about today,' said a soldier on returning from the front line. I had a patient who while manifesting no fear in the trenches or even when exposed to fire, nevertheless suffered from an extreme degree of constipation because he dared not relieve his bowels. His conscious thought was : 'If I s— (in the latrine) I shall be hit.' (Projection of the action.) Perhaps the close similarity between the word 's—' and the word 'hit' is here worthy of note. 'S—' evidently contains an affect which we wish to censor or repress, hence we use the word 'defecate'. The objectionable, anti-social affect is aggression—'hit.' The exceptional affective importance of the term is emphasised by the fact that it is the only word in this monograph which printers have refused to print.

49

manifestation is a compromise between hair and no hair in the form of patches of alopecia.

It was pointed out (end of Section III) that the normal concern over alopecia (and greyness) are displacements of castration anxiety. May it not be that this normal anxiety is well founded—upon an unconscious recognition that loss of hair is a *physical* equivalent of castration ?

Here we seem to be coming to a point where mental and physical begin to meet on common ground. As psycho-analysis reveals deeper and deeper levels of the unconscious mind it discovers mental mechanisms and laws which are so different from those of consciousness that persons acquainted only with the latter refuse to believe in these discoveries. Is it not possible that in this new region of the mind we are gradually approaching a point where mental processes begin to emerge from physical processes, the point of junction between matter and mind, or at least a point at which they are most intimately related and have a causal influence each upon the other. The man who feels sufficiently castrated in his unconscious begins to lose his hair ; the man or animal who reaches puberty (i.e. phallic maturity) grows secondary sexual characters, largely in the form of hair.

At any rate Dr. Róheim has no doubts about the matter when he writes :

'As a prototype of all the transformations to which the libido becomes subjected in the course of its long history ... stags and lions grow antlers and manes (hair) in the rutting period *because the surplus of libidinal energy recedes back from the genital organ to the whole body.*'[1]

May it not be that this is an explanation of why hair symbolises genitals ? Is it that the unconscious mind follows the physical process, and by direct experience *knows* hair to

[1] Róheim : *The International Journal of Psycho-Analysis*, Vol. XIII, Parts 1 and 2, pp. 94-95

be an expression of the libido—an id equivalent, usually a genital equivalent ?

We call the hair that grows upon the lips and jaws of man a 'secondary sexual character.' May not this be a superficial conscious recognition of the same thing ? At any rate, according to the evidence revealed by dreams, the Unconscious has no doubts whatsoever about the identity (*in source*) of penis and beard, for it constantly presents the latter when it means the former.

# SECTION VII

## *Evidence from Erotic Perversions or Fetishism*

For those who resist analytical interpretation, and even deduction, to the last ditch, it is perhaps necessary to adduce incontrovertible evidence. In hair fetishism we have such evidence—at least as far as its sexual meaning is concerned, though I think evidence of the *development* of fetishism, adduced towards the end of this section, may establish an even earlier anal source. Economy of space necessitates abbreviation, but only a few cases need be mentioned as they speak so much and so forcefully even in a brief reference.

No claim is made that hair is the only object on the conscious plane that symbolises sexuality any more than it is the only fetish. Stanley Hall says :

'There is almost no feature, article of dress, attitude, act, or even animal or perhaps object in nature that may not have to some morbid soul specialised erogenic and erethic power.'[1]

Havelock Ellis says :

'This process (the formation of the fetish) inevitably tends to take place around all those features and objects associated with the beloved person which have most deeply impressed the lover's mind, and the more sensitive and imaginative and emotional he is the more certainly will such features and objects crystallise into erotic symbols.'[2]

'Devotion and love,' wrote Mary Woolstonecraft, 'may be allowed to hallow the garments as well as the person,

[1] G. S. Hall : *Adolescence*, Vol. 1, p. 470
[2] Havelock Ellis : *Studies in the Psychology of Sex*, Vol. V, p. 9

52

for the lover must want fancy who has not a sort of sacred respect for the glove or slipper of his mistress. He would not confound them with vulgar things of the same kind.'[1]

'It is important to remember that while erotic symbolism becomes fantastic and abnormal in its extreme manifestations, it is in its essence absolutely normal."[2]

It is in particular this quality of its absolute normality which makes worthy of our study its extreme or abnormal manifestations, specifically when the symbol used is that of hair. My point is that extreme manifestations reveal in a high light the pathology of analagous normal tendencies. The equivalent normal mechanisms similarly depend on mental processes remote from reason or the ego-reality principle.

Havelock Ellis says :

"As a sexual fetish hair strictly belongs to the group of parts of the body ; but since it can be removed from the body and is sexually effective as a fetish in the absence of the person to whom it belongs, it is on a level with the garments which may serve in a similar way, with shoes or handkerchiefs or gloves."[3]

In the course of our study of some clinical material we may obtain further insight into how this particular form of fetishism arises. It is of special interest to us in that in its milder or normal forms, unrecognised as fetishistic, it is universal ; but it is sufficiently widespread in its more extreme or pathological forms to provide us with incontrovertible evidence for our thesis.

'Cases of hair fetishism which lead to attacks on female hair seem to occur everywhere from time to time.'[4]

Krafft Ebing quotes a number of cases which I shall condense and rearrange in order of their increasing patho-

[1]Havelock Ellis : *Studies in the Psychology of Sex*, Vol. V, p. 9
[2]Ibid, p. 8
[3]Ibid, p. 75
[4]Dr. R. V. Krafft Ebing : *Psychopathia Sexualis*, p. 246.

genicity. There is a gradual transition from normal admiration of a woman's hair to every degree of pathological extreme, a transition without any sharp line of demarcation, although of course instances from opposite ends of the series may appear at first sight to have little in common. This absence of any line of demarcation is indicative of identical mental mechanisms throughout the series. It may even be considered normal if a man falls in love with a woman on account of her beautiful hair, but when we get to the position of a case described by Krafft Ebing, in which the husband can only make love to his wife if she wears an immense wig with enormously long hair, it is easy to recognise that we are at a pathological stage. My point is that in the admiration or over-valuation of a person's hair we are already on the same road, however unsuspected. In the case just referred to the result of the marriage after five years was two children and a collection of 72 wigs ! The production of a family together with the innumerable articles of personal and household adornment, though normal, may scientifically be regarded as fetishistically analogous.

Case 102 is of a man between thirty and forty who could trace his attraction to female hair back to the age of eight years. In spite of sexual seduction by girls from the age of nine, he remained more sexually interested in hair than in overt sexuality. At the age of ten he began to have erotic feelings at the sight of any female hair that pleased him. So it would appear that the fetishistic idea was already established in early childhood. His desire was to touch ladies' hair, and he wrote essays and poems on its beauty. Later his desire extended from looking to kissing and sucking and he could not prevent himself from imprinting a kiss on ladies' heads when the opportunity offered in a crowd. His erotic dreams were all about hair. Later even fallen hair began to excite him. He once stole the combings of a lady's hair, put it in his mouth and masturbated while phantasying its owner.

Krafft Ebing was naturally unaware of more recent psycho-analytical theories of introjection, in the light of which these symptoms would suggest that the man had identified his mother with her hair and introjected it cannibalistically at the oral erotic stage of development. In this connection and with reference to the immediately preceding section (anal) it is interesting to recall a published case which in childhood had phantasies of obtaining control over his parents by eating their faeces.

'Infantile sadism aroused by jealousy and fear in connection with the parents' relationship is first discharged in excretory acts, urination and defecation, and at the same time (as Melanie Klein has shown) the parents' excreta and their excretory acts stand for their sexuality and are the object of the child's sexual interest. In this situation the control of the parents becomes synonymous with the control of the sadistic id impulses, which have been projected into parents, and internalised again when the parents are introjected.'[1]

Another case quoted by Krafft Ebing had at the age of fifteen erotic feelings with erection at the sight of one of the village beauties combing her hair. Later the sight of young girls with flowing hair over their shoulders always excited him intensely. He dreamt of female heads with the hair braided or flowing, never about the whole form of a woman. More recently, female hair in his fingers was sufficient to induce ejaculation. It may be worth noting that at his native place the women always wore their hair done up. This suggests to the analyst that the, to him unusual, experience of seeing the village beauty combing her hair symbolised a revelation of the hidden mystery of sexuality, in the same way as in Victorian times, when every part of the female

[1]Dr. Payne : *International Journal of Psycho-Analysis*, Vol. 20, p. 164

body was concealed, the sight of even my lady's ankles peeping from beneath her skirt might arouse sexual interest.

A more extreme case is that of a man who was arrested as he forcibly cut off a young girl's hair. He confessed that he had committed this crime on ten occasions as a result of an irresistible passion and that he took the hair home and obtained great delight from it. On searching his home sixty-five switches and tresses of hair were found sorted in packets. He confessed that when he could take a young girl's hair in his hand it produced intense sexual excitement with erection and ejaculation without touching the girl in any other way. His hair orgies were interspersed with long periods of self-imprisonment, when he shut himself up in his room for days on end. But these attempts to suppress his desires produced a state of increasing depression finally leading to another outburst and apparently a restoration of what was to him normal spirits. The act of hair despoiling had much of the significance of the sexual act for when he touched the hair with the scissors he experienced erection and at the instant of cutting it off, ejaculation. At the same time he said that at the height of this act he was in such a state of excitement that he had only imperfect apperception and subsequent recollection of what he had done.[1]

It may be as well to quote Krafft Ebing's theories of fetishism if only as an introduction to the more advanced theories of psycho-analysts. He says :

'In most individuals a sexual instinct awakes long before there is any possibility or opportunity of intimate intercourse, and the early desires of youth are concerned with the ordinary appearance of the attired female form. Thus it happens that not infrequently at the beginning of the *vita sexualis* ideas of the persons exerting sexual charms and ideas of their attire become associated. This association may be lasting—the attired woman may be

[1] Dr. R. V. Krafft Ebing : *Psychopathia Sexualis*, pp. 242-3

always preferred—if the individuals dominated by this perversion do not in other respects attain to a normal *vita sexualis*, and find gratification in natural charms.'[1]

It may be added that in accordance with our thesis the 'natural charms' may similarly be regarded as fetishistic.

With reference to the last case quoted, I am reminded of a patient of mine who differed from it only in that the fetishistic object was ladies' overcoats instead of ladies' hair. Though married he was and always had been completely impotent. He suppressed his coat-soiling and coat-slashing impulse for long periods only to experience increasing depression in spite of frequent daily masturbatings with coat phantasies. Unlike Krafft Ebing's case he could obtain satisfaction from coats without association with their owners, though he preferred the association. Though he did not obtain ejaculation during his soiling or slashing act he would obtain it at the first opportunity thereafter, masturbating and conjuring up the actual experience in phantasy. What was particularly striking was his imperfect apperception at the time and his subsequent imperfect recollection of what he had done. It occurs to one here that sexuality in general, even normal sexuality, may not be perfectly recollected during asexual phases, but only during periods when the sexual instincts are aroused. Also, from one's own clinical experience of such cases one can understand the paucity of Krafft Ebing's evidence regarding the origin of fetishism, as these cases in particular appear to have an unusually powerful amnesia not only for their infancy, but for their early childhood, indicative of the strength of repression which in turn suggests particularly traumatic castration phantasies.

Krafft Ebing was naturally unaware of this, but he says :
'One can understand how, with an intense and early sexual impression, combined with the idea of a particular

[1]Dr. R. V. Krafft Ebing : *Psychopathia Sexualis*, p. 247

garment on the woman, in hyperaesthetic individuals, a very intense interest in this garment might be developed.'[1]

What applies to garments apparently applies to hair also, though the latter is obviously nearer to, if not an actual part of, the body of the person towards whom the sexual impulse or phantasy is originally attached.

Freud considered that perversions or deviations from the adult sexual aim are to be explained as (*a*) lingering at the stage of 'fore pleasure' relations to the sexual object, or (*b*) 'anatomical transgressions of the bodily regions designed for the sexual union'. He considers this due to over-estimation : 'the substituting for a normal sexual object of another object which is related to it but which is totally unfit for the normal sexual aim.' But a particularly interesting comment for our purpose is : 'Everyday experience has shown that most of these transgressions, at least the milder ones, are seldom wanting as components in the sexual life of normals, who look upon them as upon other intimacies. Wherever the conditions are favourable such a perversion may for a long time be substituted by a normal person for the normal sexual aim, or it may be placed near it. In no normal person does the normal sexual aim lack some designatable perverse element . . .'[2] And again : 'Adult object-finding is frequently determined by fetishism ; the love-object must possess certain coloured hair, wear certain clothing, or perhaps even have certain physical blemishes. This is traceable to early impressions in connection with first object-love relationships and is quite normal. It is to be regarded as pathological if there is also a diminution in the striving for the adult sexual aim, or "when the fetish disengages itself from the person and becomes itself a sexual object".'[3] Freud points out that of the three components of the sexual impulse, its source, aim and object, the object is the most variable. 'It

[1]Dr. R. V. Krafft Ebing : *Psychopathia Sexualis*, p. 248
[2]*The Stucture and Meaning of Psycho-Analysis*, p. 99
[3]Ibid, p. 105

may be changed any number of times in the course of the vicissitudes the instinct undergoes during life.'[1] In fetishism it obviously had a very strong fixation to some early part-object, probably due to a very strong repression of something more sexually essential to which this part-object was associated. This essential could be the more easily repressed while the part-object cathected the libido normally belonging to the repressed object—and thus formed the fetish. What Krafft Ebing does not tell us and what Freud does is 'that the basis of fetishism is aversion to the real female genitals.' The basis of this, Freud insists, is the original unwelcome perception that the female does not possess a phallus—an intolerable stimulation of and confirmation of the repressed castration phantasy. The fetishist consequently seizes an advantage in a *substitute* for the genital organs of the woman ; underclothing suggests the scene of undressing, the last moment in which the woman can still be regarded as having a phallus. Velvet and fur reproduce the pubic hair which ought to have revealed the longed-for penis. This is sometimes complicated by a double attitude on the part of the fetishist : in very subtle cases the fetish becomes the vehicle of both denying and asserting the fact of castration. In this way we may understand something of the unconscious motive of hair snipping . . . finally Freud adds this : 'that in often very subtle ways the normal prototype of all fetishes is the phallus of man.'[2]

In his *Three Contributions to the Theory of Sex*, Freud showed that the fetish was a substitute for an infantile sexual object and that the selection of the fetish object was influenced by a coprophilic smell attraction.[3]

Thus we see that as early as 1905 Freud had found evidence of the anal element in the formation of fetishism. I would add that by inference this anal element must also

[1] *The Structure and Meaning of Psycho-Analysis*, p. 105
[2] Ibid, p. 404
[3] *International Journal of Psycho-Analysis*, Vol. 20, p. 161

exist in the significance of hair, one of the most favoured of fetishes. Later Freud emphasised that the fetish symbolises the penis and its presence relieved the castration fear of the male which was aroused by the sight of the female genital.[1] Abraham also has laid stress on the anal elements in the development of the fetishist. Recently Balint has stressed that the fetish 'not only symbolises a genital, male or female, but also has a faecal significance.'[2]

I may say that these points have been brought out in a paper[3] published two years after my article on the Unconscious Significance of Hair in which I stressed it could be traced beyond the genital to anal roots. So far as the genital level of fetishism goes Freud has no doubts whatsoever on the subject. He says :

'In all the cases the meaning and purpose of the fetish turned out under analysis to be the same . . . to put it plainly : the fetish is a substitute for the woman's (mother's) phallus which the little boy wants to believe in and does not wish to forgo—we know why.'[4]

The reason is that the concept of the possibility of the absence of the phallus is too provocative of castration anxiety to be tolerated in consciousness and is therefore very determinedly repressed. It is as though the infant's mind *must* see this important object somewhere in some form or another. The fetish serves that purpose. 'Something else has taken its place, has been appointed its successor, so to speak, and now absorbs all the interest which formerly belonged to the penis. But this interest undergoes yet another very strong reinforcement because the horror of castration sets up a sort of permanent memorial to itself by creating this substitute. Aversion from the real feminine genitals, which is never lacking in any fetishist, also remains as an indelible stigma of the repression that has taken place. One can now

[1]*International Journal of Psycho-Analysis*, Vol. 20, P. 161   [2]Ibid 161-162   [3]Ibid
[4]Sigmund Freud : *International Journal of Psycho-Analysis*, Vol. 9, pp. 161-162

see what the fetish achieves and how it is enabled to persist. It remains a token of triumph over the threat of castration and a safeguard against it . . .'[1]

'One would expect that the organs or objects selected as substitutes for the missing penis in the woman would be such as act as symbols for the penis in other respects.'[2] In support of the theory that the fetish itself becomes the vehicle both of denying and of asseverating the fact of castration Freud quotes a case[3] where the fetish was a suspensory belt which could also be worn as bathing drawers, and points out that this piece of clothing covers the genitals and altogether conceals the difference between those of male and female. He points out that its forerunner in childhood had been the figleaf seen on a statue, an interesting comment on normal psychology regarding this matter of the genital organ and its concealment by drawers or figleaf—or fetishistically by hair.

Like all symptoms fetishism emanates from a conflict, a conflict of two opposite tendencies. The first would be an impulse for gratification of an instinct which, if on such primitive levels as the oral or even the phallic, would involve the destruction of the object, and the second would be the later need to love and preserve the desired object. (The hair fetishist loves the woman's hair but frequently has the impulse to despoil or 'castrate' it.) This is evident in some of the cases quoted from Krafft Ebing and in my case of the overcoat fetishism to which I have referred. Freud interestingly calls attention to a 'race psychological parallel to fetishism : the Chinese custom of first mutilating a woman's foot and then revering it. The Chinese man seems to want to thank the woman for having submitted to castration.'[4] Is this so remote from the normal attitude of

[1]Sigmund Freud : *International Journal of Psycho-Analysis*, Vol. 9, p. 163
[2]Ibid, pp. 163-164
[3]Ibid, p. 165
[4]Ibid, Vol. 9, p. 165

man to woman or of the male of any mammal towards the female : the defloration and loving or even revering ?

In contrast to the abundance of cases of fetishism in males the literature on the subject is extraordinarily barren regarding the presence, or even the possibility, of fetishism in *women*. I have not succeeded in discovering the publication of a single case. Whereas the psychopathology of male fetishism appears to rest upon an anxiety-provoking disappointment in discovering an absence of the phallus in the woman, primarily in the mother, and thereupon making good the inconceivable loss by substitution of the fetish, the psychopathology of woman's equivalent interest would seem to be in procuring an infinite number of phallic substitute objects with which to make good her loss. The socially permissible narcissism of the woman is perhaps a recognition and acceptance of the fact that in the absence of husband or child she requires, needs, the fetishistic substitute in the form of her own person. Apart from the fetishistic value of her body as a whole and her hair in particular, every one of her personal ornaments from her high-heeled shoes to the feather at the top of her hat is first and last a fetishistic substitute for her missing phallus.

But more important, or at least more fundamental than this method of substitution, is that which is pre-cultural and even biogenic. It is the acquisition of the phallic substitute in the form of the male, his phallus, and perhaps even more important, the baby, which is more indisputably her own possession, her own 'phallus'.

Here perhaps we get to the psychopathological progenitor of ordinary male fetishism. A woman analyst has pointed out to me that this civilisation abounds in mothers who, not content to produce a son as their much-wanted phallic substitute, proceed to cling to him as they would to a phallus which they were for ever in danger of losing. Their anxiety is expressed, or in a sense compensated for, by a firm, immovable hold upon the phallic object which they have made, and inadvertently almost lost. Fathers are inclined to allow mothers to maintain this life-long stranglehold upon their son presumably because they accept the fact that the woman has produced him and they do not care, or are psychologically incapable of appreciating, that she is now smothering his capacity for normal development. 'They go bad on you if you keep them,' was my remark to a mother who shamelessly expressed the hope that her grown-up son would never leave her.

No father could socially if not familially succeed in an equal degree of possession and seduction of a daughter without being suspected of incest. Thus we see that if fetishism as such does not exist in women, an analogous trend manifesting itself both culturally in the accumulation of substitutive objects, such as personal ornaments, and biologically in the need for phallic equivalents such as husband and children, is the rule rather than the exception and is rightly regarded as a normal manifestation of feminine psychology. We see further that at least one practising analyst considers that fetishism as manifested in men has its deepest origin in the castration anxiety of their mothers.

To revert to our specific subject, hair : it may be relevant to recall that it is customary to allow women but not men to grow their hair long, implying possibly a compensatory indulgence, compensatory for the phantasied genital castration.

In accordance with more recent developments of psycho-analytical theory, the interpretation of fetishism in general, and therefore by implication of hair fetishism, has been carried a stage further. 'It has been recognised that libidini-sation of the penis imago is the basis of ego development, and at this phase it represents the ego. I think the erect position attained in standing in infancy and erection of the penis have comparable narcissistic values, and that castration fears are associated with a threat to either . . . every component of the infantile sexual instinct has some connection with the fetish object, so that this object is associated with all the repressed infantile sexual experiences.'[1]

'The relationship of a man to his fetish is the same as his relationship to his internalised parents . . . The fetish reanimates the pre-genital substitutes for genital sexuality, and also provides special defences against the aggression of pre-genital sexuality.'[2]

'The fetish can stand for the father's penis or the woman's genital, nipple, body, anal tract, or the parents' faeces.'[3] 'The fetish stands for part objects which have been eaten and also preserved . . . this internalised object is projected into the fetish, the latter represents the loved object and the super-ego . . . In common with other fetishes it is a real external object and as a substitute for a love-object denotes an effort to find contact with an external object and externalise an internal conflict . . . I think that the fetish defence denotes that libidinal development has attempted to pass the anal phases, and that the phallic phase is partially reached . . . The fetish representing as it does a combination of part objects, the combined parents represented by their faeces, and also in many situations the father's penis, stands for a good introjected object.'[4]

'Klein's work on depressed states and their connection with an early phase of ego development is supported by the analysis of the psychical background of the individual who has the necessity for a fetish.'[5]

What the author does not add is that we all in some degree or other have the most abundant necessity for innumerable fetishes. A real apprehension of the causes of

[1]Dr. Payne : *International Journal of Psycho-Analysis*, Vol. 20, p. 166
[2]Ibid, p. 167    [3]Ibid
[4]Ibid, Vol. 20, p. 168
[5]Ibid, p. 169

this sexual phenomenon can only be obtained by considering the fetish in its relation to the individual's whole psychical development and by taking into account the several morbid symptoms which are invariably present. The author goes on to say, and this statement (though questionable regarding the comparative quantity of anxiety-guilt), summarises the mechanism, and in its main outline coincides with my view : 'The fetishist has much more conscious anxiety and guilt than an individual with an established perversion, and in this respect resembles the psycho-neurotic. The over-determination of the fetish both from the point of view of sexuality and ego defence can be compared to that of a neurotic symptom. In common with phobia the mechanism of projection and displacement is used and a substitute object is selected, but there is a reversal of affect, as the object is to attract not to repel.'[1]

The universality of hair fetishism may be brought into relief by this short instance of its negative aspect : A young woman patient of mine who had become completely bald, although most broad-minded on all conventional issues had an indescribable horror of her predicament being seen or even suspected by anybody. It caused her to relinquish her employment for fear of discovery and to forgo a romantic love-attachment because discovery would in due course have become inevitable. She felt quite 'incompatible' with any man's loving or desiring her. She thought the absence of an arm or a leg would not be so bad.

Her attitude is perhaps a fair comment upon the universality of hair fetishism or the general overvaluation of hair.

If we care for the sake of emphasis and clarity to speak just a little loosely, the incredible reply to the incredulous question 'Is everything sexual?' would be 'No, on the contrary, everything is a fetish.' We are all fetishists, and

[1] *International Journal of Psycho-Analysis*, Vol. 20, p. 169

that is why, like them, we resist recognition of the source of our current substitutive interests. Our hair preoccupations are just one instance of this generalisation. The important point is not that hair can, like shoes or overcoats, become a sexual symbol, but that unlike these objects it has practically no other significance in our present-day life. It has ceased to be the 'overcoat' provided by nature against the elements, but it has not ceased to be of psychological, as distinct from physical, significance ; and this psychological significance is predominantly sexual as is startlingly revealed by the phenomenon of hair fetishism and less startlingly, only by dint of usage, by the phenomenon of all our normal hair behaviour, and attitudes, customs and conventions.

To sum up : there is no denying the existence of the startling phenomenon of hair fetishism. The existence of such a phenomenon is itself, without argument, direct proof that hair, not only can, but actually does, undeniably in some instances, assume the role of a sexual symbol. Evidence and conclusion are here complete without the necessity for any theorising. The theory of the mental mechanism whereby hair in certain instances assumes such an all-important role as a fetishistic sexual object begins with Krafft Ebing's commonsense deduction that fetishism proceeds from some early, possibly infantile, association of an object (any object) with the sexually desired object or person. The emphasis is as it were switched from the original sexual object on to the associated substitute. The substitute then survives while the original sexual object is forgotten.

Psycho-analysis goes a step further to show why such a phenomenon should take place in such a marked degree. It tells us that the original sexual object at these early stages of infantile development was in the case of the boy the phallus presumed to be possessed by his mother. The fetish was as it were the last object he could perceive while he still maintained the illusion of his mother's possession of a phallus. Going beyond that object he made the significant discovery that there was no phallus. On account of his castration anxiety he was quite unable to tolerate the concept of their being no phallus. He therefore decided that this last object, commonly clothing or hair, was the sought-for and insisted-upon phallus. He therefore clung to this, principally to cover the concept of castration as the anxiety associated with such a concept was to him quite intolerable. At the same time the aggressive elements of his sexual instinct included the impulse to perform himself this castration (cf. defloration and active masculine sexual impulse); hence the hair-despoiling or hair-cutting element so frequently present.

More recently some analysts have pushed the theory of fetishism in general a little further in keeping with Melanie Klein's concept of introjection connected with the pre-genital organisations of the libido on an oral and anal plane.

For our purpose in this paper the phenomenon of hair fetishism is important for two reasons : one, that in these extreme cases it proves the erotic symbolism of hair without theory or argument ; and two, because no normal person is without some degree of this particular form of fetishism. Many normal persons, particularly men, have even gone so far as to allow their hair fetishism to be the chief determining factor in their process of sexual selection.

# *Application of these Theories to some Additional Material*

IN the light of these observations and the tentative theories based upon them, a number of phenomena connected with the psychology of hair-affect and hair-behaviour present themselves to us and demand to be taken into consideration.

I cannot hope to deal with these matters exhaustively or even systematically and shall therefore content myself with a few brief notes.

Affects connected with the colour of hair :

The popular interest in *red* hair is revealed by the dream associations of analysands to be due to the closer resemblance of a head-top of this *colour* to the glans penis or vulva. (I have already pointed out that a dream-figure conspicuous for its hair is a genital symbol, *vide* footnote page 48.) Thus a hysterical woman patient nearing the transference stage of analysis dreams of her analyst (dark haired) as having erect, red hair. Attempts to associate to this produce the utmost confusion, blushings and finally tears and hysteria. Interpretation leads to screaming and fierce denials. But at subsequent sessions the correctness of the interpretation is admitted. A male patient of characterological type in relating a dream of a red-headed figure, had no hesitation in describing it in these words : 'Red—like the top of the penis.' The reaction of many unanalysed readers to these clinical excerpts is liable to be of a quality intermediate between the two though often approximating more to that of the first-mentioned patient.

The popular idea that red-headed people are gifted with a super-normal capacity for detumescence possibly has its chief cause in this unconscious association. Medical evidence would seem to show that they are at least as frequently cursed with a super-normal capacity for rheumatism, chorea or tuberculosis.

*Darkness or blackness* of the hair (as every other colour attribute of hair) is not without its significance for the unconscious. Though here a preference for it, at least in males, seems to be supported by the observation that pigmentation is related to the sexual development as well as to the actual sexual centres. Thus Havelock Ellis tells us that the degree of pigmentation is clearly correlated with sexual vigour and that at puberty as well as at pregnancy there is a general tendency to changes in pigmentation.[1]

[1]Havelock Ellis : *Studies in the Psychology of Sex*, Vol. V, pp. 191-3
'The degree of pigmentation is clearly correlated with sexual vigour. "In general," Heusinger laid down, in 1823, "the quantity of pigment is proportional to the functional effectiveness of the genital organs." This connection is so profound that it may be traced very widely throughout the organic world.
'The connection between pigmentation and sexual activity is very ancient. Even leaving out of account the wedding apparel of animals, nearly always gorgeous in scales and plumage and hair, the sexual orifice shows a more or less marked tendency to pigmentation during the breeding season from fishes upward, while in mammals the darker pigmentation of this region is a constant phenomenon in sexually mature individuals.
'In the human species both the negative standard of castration and the positive standard of puberty alike indicate a correlation of this kind. Those individuals in whom puberty never fully develops and who are consequently said to be affected by infantilism, reveal a relative absence of pigment in the sexual centres which are normally pigmented to a high degree. Among those Asiatic races who extirpate the ovaries in young girls the skin remains white in the perineum, round the anus and in the armpits. Even in mature women who undergo ovariotomy, as Kepler found, the pigmentation of the nipples and areolae disappears, as well as of the perineum and anus, the skin taking on a remarkable whiteness.
'Normally the sexual centres, and in a high degree the genital orifice, represent the maximum of pigmentation, and under some circumstances this is clearly visible even in infancy. Thus babies of mixed black and white blood may show no traces of negro ancestry at birth, but there will always be increased pigmentation about the external genetalia. The linea fusca, which reaches from the pubes to the navel and ocasionally to the ensiform cartilage, is a line of sexual pigmentation sometimes regarded as characteristic of pregnancy, but as Andersen, of Copenhagen, has found by the examination of several hundred children of both sexes, it exists in a slight form in about 75 per cent. of young girls, and in almost as large a proportion of boys. But there is no doubt that it tends to increase with age as well as to become marked at pregnancy. At puberty there is a general tendency to changes in pigmentation ; thus Godin found that in 28 per cent. adolescent changes occurred in the eyes and hair at this period, the hair becoming darker, though the eyes sometimes become lighter. Ammon, in his investigation of conscripts at the age of 20, discovered the significant fact that the eyes and hair darken *pari passu* with sexual development. In women,

It may be that the frequent preference for *fair hair* in women ('Gentlemen prefer Blondes') may be in keeping with an ideal of their passive role in the sexual situation. The male commonly prefers that which is least virile, least 'masculine', in his choice of sexual partner.

I consider that another element here is a preference for 'cleanliness'. The fair person, or the fair hair, seems 'cleaner' and therefore does not so strongly disturb or mobilise anal-erotic reaction formations. In any case sexual attraction is apt to encounter anal-erotic reaction formations (cf. such expressions as 'dirty dog', and a common idea that sex is 'dirty'), and where this might occur to the extent of destroying the attraction in the case of dark, 'dirty' or brown hair it may be escaped where the hair is fair and 'clean' looking. This association of fair hair and cleanness or purity is supported by the examples quoted in the section on Folklore.

*Long hair* may be attractive or may be repulsive according to whether the subject of the emotion is disposed to enjoy or repudiate the penis-substitute. A great number of complications here enter into the subjective attitude. For example as Flugel has pointed out[1] long hair can obviously have two opposite meanings : (*a*) (probably primary) masculine—where long hair means much penis, and (*b*) feminine ;

during menstruation, there is a general tendency to pigmentation ; this is especially obvious around the eyes, and in some cases black rings of true pigment form in this position. Even the skin of the negro women of Loango sometimes becomes a few shades darker during menstruation. During pregnancy this tendency to pigmentation reaches its climax. Pregnancy constantly gives rise to pigmentation of the face, the neck, the nipples, the abdomen, and this is especially marked in brunettes.

'This association of pigmentation and sexual aptitudes has been recognised in the popular lore of some peoples. Thus the Sicilians, who admire brown skin and have no liking either for a fair skin or light hair, believe that a white woman is incapable of responding to love. It is the brown woman who feels love.'

Nevertheless, I am convinced that the primary causative factor in pigmentation is climatic, specifically solar. I am convinced also that it operates phylogenetically through a neo-Lamarckian process of evolution. If it is correlated with increased sexual vigour, the actinic rays of the sun may be given the credit for this also. However, it should be remembered that we are here concerned with subjective attitudes and not with objective realities as such.

[1] J. C. Flugel : *Psychology of Clothes*, p. 109

because by social convention women have for many years worn longer hair than men. Hence the *secondary* association to long hair, brought about by social usage is feminine—i.e. no penis. In modern times we see that homosexual (i.e. feminine) men tend therefore to wear long hair and homosexual (i.e. masculine) women short hair.

This was not always the case. The struggle of the early seventeenth century between the Cavaliers and Roundheads is an interesting representation of the conflict between sexual libido and super-ego. The Cavaliers, who wore their hair long, indulged in women and wine and generally expressed their libidinous impulses. The Roundheads, who cut their hair short, were Puritans—symbolically and mentally they cut off their penis—albeit they assumed a substitutive and compensatory aggression. It is noteworthy that Cavaliers and Roundheads were in conflict.[1]

In modern times it seems that the fashion is to emphasise this puritanical erotic castration in the case of men, whereas (as was mentioned earlier) women, who have no penis, are permitted by society to wear long hair ; it is not offensive in them. As would be expected the extreme cases of this puritanical reaction against the penis, or against long hair, are to be found in the celibate religious orders. Hence we observe that monks and nuns shave their heads apparently in the endeavour to achieve asexuality. This is not the only possible way in which extreme asceticism can be expressed in hair-behaviour, for we see that the extreme ascetics of India, the Fakirs, simply ignore altogether the very existence of their hair (cf. the ascetic tendency to ignore the existence of the genital organs). It grows into a matted lice-inhabited mass and may almost be as much a source of unremitting torment as the neglected penis itself. Apparently it is not permitted to exist as far as *consciousness* is concerned.[2]

[1] Milton, the only important Puritan poet, wore his hair long.

[2] It is noteworthy that in the Fakir cult almost every organ and part of the body is focused under conscious attention and control *with the striking exception of the genital organs*.

These various antitheses between the enjoyment of long hair and the hatred or repudiation of it are not so bewildering in the light of the genital-sexual conflict. For here it is common knowledge that pleasure and repudiation (or horror) alternately win the day.

My male patient whose sexual libido had in infancy been frightened away from heterosexuality, enjoys moderately long hair in his young male love-objects and becomes almost ill if one of them appears with his hair recently cut short. Apparently the association of the short hair to castration is too painful for him. Similar elements enter into his horror of the (castrated) female.

Women who like the male's hairiness (e.g. men with beards) are commonly highly heterosexual and not averse to the male sexual organ, while scruples in this respect commonly imply sexual scruples also.

A dislike of long hair should perhaps be distinguished from a dislike of *untidy hair*. The latter may well be due to the provocation of anal-erotic reaction-formations.

In connection with the subject of untidy hair we may consider the affects produced by hair out of place, in the sense of hair on other parts of the body. It may be felt to be untidy to have hair where we do not ordinarily expect it, or where we are not consciously amenable to its acceptance. I here quote from Malinowski. Referring to the Trobirand Islanders he says :

'Hair in its proper place is considered a great beauty, but as we know, it must not be allowed to grow anywhere except on the scalp. Eyebrows are shaved off, the beard is never allowed to grow except by old men "who do not wish to have anything to do with women". The hair on the head is admired when it is very full and then it is allowed to grow into a thick mop of which almost every hair radiates from the scalp, in the manner so characteristic of Melanesia.'[1]

And again:

'*Body hair is regarded as ugly and is kept shaven*, only in myth and in fairy tale do certain people appear who are covered with unu' unu; to the natives a grotesque and at the same time a perverse characteristic.'[2]

But perhaps it is unnecessary to look as far as Melanesia for illustrations of the powerful affects connected with untidy or misplaced hair. Any hair-dresser or beauty specialist will tell us of her modern English clients whose lives are made miserable by the growth of even a few adventitious hairs on face or chin or other odd place where they feel they ought not to be. Indeed the client can justify her misery and alarm, for it is not only her own personal affect that is involved but also that of every person with whom she comes into contact, including those upon whose affection and esteem her well-being may depend. A husband's affections may easily be alienated by so trivial a thing as the growth of a few sporadic hairs on that part of his wife's lip which he formerly loved to kiss. That which to him was lovely has become repulsive. Why? The answer is that these affects are not based upon reality values, but like all the affects connected with hair, have their source in those unconscious constellations which we are endeavouring to plumb. In keeping with the theory formed on the basis of our clinical material, we may hazard a guess that the distressing tuft of hair which grows upon my lady's cheek is the blatant revelation of the cloven hoof, devil's tail, or *penis*, showing through the otherwise spotless white garment of purity.[3] Hair *in the right place* we may have accepted as a

[1]Malinowski: *Sexual Life of Savages*, p. 252
[2]Ibid, p. 253
[3]In Tolstoi's *War and Peace* the little princess, wife of Prince Andrew Bolkonski, had a light down on her upper lip, and this is mentioned several times by the author as one of her principal sources of attractiveness. Apparently the down was so light as to carry associations to infantile, and therefore guiltless, genitals.

73

desirable object, carrying its pleasure affect from the otherwise repressed genital levels ; but if we are confronted with hair, such as pubic hair which *too* consciously suggests the *source* of our ordinary hair pleasure, all the repudiation and horror unconsciously associated with the original struggle of the emergence of the ego from its libidinal enemy is then provoked.

Axillary (arm-pit) hair is commonly shaved off by women if it is liable to exposure (e.g. in evening dress) for no other reason than that it is liable to arouse affects associated with pubic hair. While feeling the affect they are unlikely, unless analysed, to appreciate its source.

*Erect hair* is obviously symbolical of the erect penis, and the observer's reaction to it will bear a resemblance to his reaction to genital erection. Pleasure or displeasure will be experienced according to whether a positive or negative attitude in connection with genital erection predominates—with this difference, of course, namely, that where the pleasure affect relating to erect penis may be repressed to the extent of being repudiated in its conscious sexual relationship, it may still be consciously experienced as an affect in connection with erect *hair*. If the repressing forces are still more powerful, the pleasure affect may be repudiated even in this new displacement so that erect hair becomes repugnant. Again the Melanesians provide us with a good example of the positive affects. To re-quote Malinowski, 'The hair on the head is admired when it is very full, and then it is allowed to grow into a thick mop of which almost every hair radiates (erect) from the scalp in the manner so characteristic of Melanesia.'[1] Modern society commonly provides us with examples of the negative affects. There is a tendency for civilised man to brush his hair down flat, and even to guard against the contingency of erection by using various pastes or creams. As one of my

[1] Malinowski: *The Sexual Life of Savages*, p. 252

patients in his association to his dream says : 'It is rather a low-down business, not the sort of hair that stamps a member of the upper classes. Makes me think of the Bill Sykes' type of individual—anti-social.'[1] It is anti-social to go about with an erection, whether it be of the hair or of the penis, for this is the weapon with which in our repressed (flattened-down) Oedipus phantasy, we murder the father (society) and rape-murder the mother.

*Curly hair.* Much of what has been said about erect hair can be applied with modifications to curly hair. In the first place curly hair is partly erect, but has this advantage : it shows a little modesty in not being quite erect and generally more tidy. The essential association to curly hair is however a direct one to the curly hair of the pubic region. It is noteworthy that women generally have a greater preference for it, whether in males or females, than have men. One would expect women to appreciate erection in another person, provided the erection is sufficiently modest, tidy and controlled, and through its displacement unlikely to arouse sexual conflict. Men with naturally curly hair are often at pains to keep it brushed flat, as though it would be a public disgrace.

*Soft hair* may be preferred partly at least on account of its implicit insistence, that it, after all, is *not* pubic hair.

Possibly enough has been said of our behaviour in regard to our hair—what we do with it and why. It has been pointed out that we cannot leave it alone, we are always doing something with it. The act of combing or brushing our hair occasionally occurs in dreams and is associated to as a masturbation equivalent. We stroke a dog or a cat to give ourselves and the animal pleasure feeling. In one of the dreams recorded, the analyst was dreamt of as stroking or massaging the patient's (dreamer's) hair.[2] The process

[1]This paper. Clinical material. Section III
[2]Ibid.

continued until a white froth appeared. The patient's association to this was 'semen'. It is likely that affects from the same unconscious source are largely responsible for our hair activities, including the use of the shampoo.

When we attend, preserve, or love our hair, we are expressing in displaced form our appreciation of, and pleasure in, our genital sexuality. When we remove, cut, or control our hair we are giving expression to reaction formations against the genital (and anal) libido. Both forms of activity are necessary to express both sides of the sexual conflict. Are we then doomed to a slavish obedience to our unconscious? Various attempts have been made to deal with the conflict once for all. These attempts also can be shown to be blind obedience to the unconscious complex possessed by the particular individual. For example monks who shave their heads are expressing that determined castration and renunciation of rivalry with the Father which is also expressed in their beliefs and other ceremonial behaviour. In our civilisation where the masculine convention of shaving predominates, hair may be allowed to grow on the face either as a mark of masculine aggression unafraid to show itself (e.g. amongst military men) or as an attempt to compensate and make amends for unconscious feelings of femininity. Though the beard is commonly associated with gruff-voiced masculinity, many men who grow beards have shrill voices and other stigmata of femininity—cf. the bejewelled man. In such cases the beard is a compensation for unconscious castration, that is to say a reinstatement of the penis. The beard not only insists upon their masculinity but also probably gratifies their unconscious femininity, for the appearance of the mouth is then commonly associated with that of the vulva surrounded by hair.[1]

[1] It is noteworthy that in the Army while the moustache is encouraged, super-ego or castration forces are still exercised in the taboo on the beard. In the Navy, on the other hand, with the prolonged exclusion of feminine society (while at sea) the homosexuality of the band of males permits the revelation of bisexuality in the form of the beard.

The growth of a beard may also, of course, be a gesture of rebellion against, or emancipation from, the castrating trammels of convention—e.g. in artists.

Mr. Reynolds' recent, witty book on beards may serve to remind us that the subject can still release a surprising quantity of repressed libidinal energy in the form of humour, the source of which I have endeavoured to make plain.

When he tells us that Henry I and his barons submitted to having their beards chopped off in church after hearing a sermon *against the wickedness of wearing them*, we now know that the 'wickedness' of wearing beards is the wickedness in the eyes of the Church (super-ego) of exhibiting even a *secondary* sexual character, of permitting the phallus (displaced affect on to beard) to flaunt itself even in this modified form. No doubt all the other instances annotated, including all the various and varying attitudes of mind, modes of behaviour and styles of beard, can be understood only as expressions of the varying fortunes of the unconscious battle between the forces of displaced libidinal expression, and the opposing forces of suppression or annihilation, with compromises in the form of modification and control.

When furs and fur-coats appear in dreams they are practically always, in common with furry animals, symbols (*via* pubic hair) of genital organs. It is noteworthy that in our society it is customary for women only to exhibit this 'genital symbol' in common with their permitted exhibition of long hair, jewellery and other fetishistic penis substitutes.

This may bring us to a brief enumeration of various symbols which, though essentially genital, produce this association through the intermediary of hair.

Grass, foliage and bushes very commonly occur in dreams of analysands, and almost invariably have an association with hair, generally directly with pubic hair. I have a patient who is constantly dreaming of peering through bushes into a beautiful garden which he longs to enter, but there amongst the grass he sees the proverbial snake. This patient's degree of fixation to his mother is so strong as to make him almost psychotic. He is frequently on the verge of suicide in his desire to re-enter the womb (the beautiful garden). The surrounding bushes he associates with pubic hair (his mother's). The snake in the grass is of course his father's penis within. The relation of this patient's dream to the legend of the Garden of Eden leads us to regard this as the product of similar factors in the unconscious. In the frequently occurring dreams of landscapes and the associations which reveal them as mother symbols, we are apt to overlook the fact that the grass or foliage of these landscapes are maternal hair, and maternal pubic hair.

The bullrushes of the Moses story are clearly the pubic hair from which the child emerges.[1]

To come a little nearer to the present day, the Christmas Tree has been associated with hair and with father's penis. We see Father Christmas (with his long beard) taking off the toy penises that he benevolently gives to the children. (At the feast, the phylogenetic successor of the old totem feasts, his penis is eaten in the shape of an appropriate symbol— turkey or goose.)

The Gorgon's head clearly shows us that hair equals snakes equals phallus.

Samson was castrated symbolically by a woman, as so many of my heterosexually inhibited patients have feared that the woman would castrate them.

The use of *scents* is not confined to the hair, but the hair seems to be specially chosen for scenting purposes, e.g. hair lotions, oils, shampoos. The men of Southern Europe have not the horror felt by Englishmen at the use of scent on their persons, and are often heavily perfumed, making use of scent on the hair. Is this because they are somewhat less

[1]Sigmund Freud : 'Moses and Monotheism,' *International Journal of Psycho-Analysis*, Vol. IX, p. 1.

repressed, particularly as regards more primitive aspects of sexuality ?

What is the explanation of this tendency to scent the hair ? This may raise the whole question of odours and the subject of their effect upon us. In the first place nature provided bodily odours. These were originally attractive, and still are at lower levels of evolution. Odours are bound up with sexual life in many of the lower animals. Insects and fishes depend upon them for the finding of their mate. They are blindly led or impelled sexually by the odour. Stags and does excrete special sexual odours during the breeding season. We may expect to find that *homo sapiens* is no exception to the general biological rule. And we do find that it is so, at least in the lower or less conscious levels of the mind

I had a very average male analysand who spoke much during analysis of the ecstatic and sexually stimulating qualities of a mild odour of perspiration in the women with whom he danced. It was their natural bodily odour that so stimulated him. Groddeck goes so far as to say that falling in love depends upon smell.[1] It is interesting to note that the patient referred to, ceased to find his lady's odour attractive if it became a little too strong. He then experienced the familiar disgust and repulsion.

The conclusion to be drawn from this and other material is not far to seek : at some level of the unconscious these natural smells are still loved and have erotic value ; but the point arises at which conflict is provoked and more recent levels of the mind repress and repudiate. It is at this point, or rather at a point in development corresponding to this that artificial scents are introduced. The affect originally belonging to the bodily, or more specifically, the sexual odour, is then displaced on to the artificial scent, and can

[1]Georg Groddeck : *The Unknown Self*, p. 55. 'Even the most learned of men has to let his sense of smell decide for him in all his love-affairs.'

there be enjoyed without usually encountering the opposition of the repressing forces. Compare the mechanism of fetishism, and surely *the erotic enjoyment of artificial scents is an instance of a normal fetish*.[1] For our present purpose it is important to notice that the hair is the region chosen for scenting purposes. The smell of the genitals during their breeding season is sufficiently agreeable for stags and does : with human beings it is the (artificial) scent of my lady's tresses.

The connection of odour with genital sexuality is far from being its earliest, or even its most important significance. Developmentally odour is first associated with the mother's milk. Its later connection with faeces at the anal level, is one which is so strong and so important as to maintain a considerable degree of fixation throughout the whole of life. The repulsive effect produced by unduly strong bodily odours is essentially due to the reaction-formation against the *anal* level of erotism. This and other evidence helps to convince us that the pleasure affects connected with bodily smells, and in due course with artificial scents, also largely have their source at the level of positive anal-erotic pleasure. Thus through the consideration of the pleasure value of the *scent* of hair we are led not only to the discovery that hair has genital significance but even further back to the important associations with the pre-genital anal level.

Thus we see that the quantity of data regarding hair appears to be inexhaustible and depicts many aspects of unconscious conflicting elements. However, the value of annotation should not be over-estimated. The observed phenomena of nature or of culture, like the *manifest content*

---

[1] A male patient who had repressed his sexuality to a far greater extent than the one just quoted, and whose sexual object was in fact a particular young man, was in the habit of surreptitiously entering the cloakroom at his office, securing his love-object's hat, and rubbing his finger quickly around the rim. He would then beat a rapid retreat with feelings of guilt greater than that of any thief or murderer, but in the thrilling possession upon his finger of the odour of his loved one's hair oil, with which he would delight and sexually stimulate himself for the greater part of the day.

of dreams, have little or no meaning until their source or *latent content* is revealed. In the same way, a list of symptoms in an illness means little until we discover the underlying pathology. It is only then that we have a common denominator, a knowledge of the origin or source of the various phenomena, and frequently of the mechanism of their production. It is only then that we can hope to understand their meaning. What was previously a series of incomprehensible observations or events can now be integrated with the body of our knowledge, and related to its developmental past, its dynamic present, and its predictable future.

The significance or meaning of our activities and attitudes is therefore a different order of knowledge from mere annotation. It is this significance with regard to hair activities and attitudes that I am endeavouring to elucidate in the present work.

# *The Source and Mechanism of Normal Hair-Behaviour*

A GOOD deal of the psychology or psycho-pathology of hair-behaviour has come to light in the course of our considerations under the preceding sections.

If we now attempt the task of correlating, systematising or re-stating our theories in an orderly fashion we are faced with the choice of several alternative schemata of classification. On closer inspection we find that no scheme will permit us to be faithfully systematic. Let us take consolation in the thought that it is better to be faithful to the facts than faithful to any chosen system.

If we choose, for example, to discuss psycho-pathology under the functions of the Ego, the Super-ego and the Id, we find that under each of these divisions of the mind the other two insistently intrude. This is unfortunate for our desire to be orderly, but in this very misfortune we have revealed to us the essential fact of psychological research. *The fact is just this intrusion of the Id and Super-ego into the domain of the Ego.* Bearing this in mind we may with less dissatisfaction embark upon the attempt.

## *The Ego*

What has the ego to do with our hair-behaviour? A great deal. It may be the id which causes us to grow hair, and it may be the super-ego which prompts us to cut or shave it, but it is the ego which is ultimately responsible for an adjustment between these two on the one hand and environmental reality on the other.

Ask any person the cause of his individual hair-behaviour and the answer will be in terms of its ego-psychology. His ego says he must do what society expects of him. Mental economy makes for following a social custom rather than for thinking about it. So he cuts his hair and shaves his beard and is none the worse for it—except for the loss of time and the disadvantages enumerated in Section II of this paper. Indeed he feels better for it. In assessing the reason for feeling better the ego will lay stress on conforming to social usage and will of course omit those factors of which it is unaware, namely that he feels better because he thus (in his hair-behaviour) deals with the Unconscious Conflict between Id and Super-ego without unduly embarrassing his Ego—*that is to say by a symptom (hair-behaviour) rather than by a character change.*

Custom and usage may blind us to the fact that this hair-behaviour is indeed a symptom, rather than an essential ego-reality behaviour, until we are faced with unusual manifestations of it. For example, it is easy to detect something beyond the borders of ego-function in the Melanesian hair-combing ritual,[1] or without looking so far afield, in the case of the lady (and there are many) who is plunged into an anxiety state by the discovery that her carefully plucked eyebrows of single-hair width are being menaced by the growth of another row of hairs. Beauty specialists are accustomed to these alarums.

In addition to its function of adapting the individual to his environment (in which term of course is included social environment) a function of the ego is to defend itself against id demands. Is it true that the ego, if it did nothing

[1] "Hair dressing plays a great part in the personal toilet. Trimming is done by means of a sharpened mussel shell and the hair is cut off in tufts against a piece of wood. It is combed or teased with a long-pronged wooden comb, and one of the most important types of beauty magic is done over the comb. Teasing out the hair is the centre of certain festivals (kayana) which are really organised solely for the display of this beauty."
Malinowski: *The Sexual Life of Savages*, p. 253

83

about it, would be overwhelmed by the id's insistent growth of hair? Must the ego in order to survive be everlastingly directing the scissors or razor against the id's hair? Or is it *not* really *hair* that the ego shaves, cuts and controls but rather some old-time enemy never wholly vanquished, of which hair serves as the symbol, much as the national flag serves in international warfare?[1]

In so far as the ego is wasting its defensive energy against a harmless intruder its function is a morbid one, however widely adopted by society.

No matter how severe the ego may appear to be in its defensive control of this misplaced libido, it shows a corresponding leniency in its dealings with those aggressive components of the id which have gone over to the super-ego. The super-ego is permitted by the ego to attack the libidinal hair in a variety of more or less violent ways, from shaving and plucking at one end of the scale to scenting and shampooing at the other.

### Super-ego

It seems likely that another and more complicated mechanism has also taken place in this connection. We know that the whole person becomes a symbolic representation of

[1] 'An important object associated with this vendetta is the kuru-urkna (soul essence), *the girdle made of the dead man's hair*, by virtue of which the leader of the revenge expedition is assured of the protection of the dead. While the leader of the expedition presses this girdle against the stomachs of his followers, he kneels before each man in succession and each man masturbates him though not to the point of ejaculation. The Yumu call the same things manjunuma. The dead man's uncle cuts his hair, his brother puts the string into his mouth and then stretches it to each man's navel in order to stop excessive grief. They also believe that the manjunuma makes them invincible and with its help they are sure to kill the culprit.

The general function of the kuru-urkna is very similar to that of the churunga. Both are sacred objects which no woman is allowed to see, both represent a bond of goodwill between the men, and both are connected with certain moral obligations. They are both something that corresponds to the flag of the nation, something for which men will fight. Whilst the kuru-urkna is the token of the identification with the dead man, it seems also to be, in some sense, identical with the culprit, for when the kuru-urkna is torn to pieces, the victim of the expedition dies.'—Róheim: 'Central Australian Psychology,' *International Journal of Psycho-Analysis*, Vol. XIII, pp. 113-4

the phallus, and the narcissism or love of the self (including love of the ego) diverts genital libido from its usual object. We know that pleasure in one's own hair is clearly one of the manifestations of this narcissism. And now we can see the cutting of this hair not only as super-ego versus libido but as an attack by the super-ego upon the ego itself, albeit an ego that has dared to have hair (i.e. phallus). The tortures inflicted in the Neuroses by the super-ego upon the ego are here performed in a social hair-symptom instead.

We may interpret this hair cutting as the original parental castrations now taken up with diligent and repetitive insistence by the super-ego (the parent successor), or we may choose to delve to a level deeper than that of the Oedipus Complex and detect here the death impulse barely disguised as aggression and repetition. For it is not only aggression (of super-ego) against aggressive libido (hair) that we may detect, but destructive aggression against the narcissism of the whole self. Through narcissistic mechanisms the phallus has now become the self (hair) and it is this which we are destroying (death-impulse) with our cuttings and shavings.

Perhaps it should be a matter for commendation of the ego that such primitive and powerful instinct drives have been so skilfully deflected into such a harmless field of conflict.

In considering the forces arrayed against the free expression of primitive instincts in their displaced (*hair*) position, we need not confine ourselves to super-ego structure. There were forces, perhaps earlier than the super-ego, which forced the energy of these instincts from their primitive erotogenic locus to their displaced (hair) position. But neither the primitive instinctive drives nor their opponents have expended their respective energies in this first encounter. In as much as we have seen the former (i.e. instincts) in the positive aspects of our hair-behaviour we can even more readily discern the latter (repressive forces) in the negative behaviour, the anxiety and the reaction-formations connected with our hair preoccupation.

The early reaction-formations against Oedipus wishes obtain their expression in several ways. First of all the very fact of *displacement* from the genital level on to the hair is evidence of conflict against positive genital Oedipus wishes. Reaction-formations are shown in the ritual of cutting the hair—as one of my patients expressed it 'to please the woman'. It is as if the little Oedipus conceived of his hair (phallus) as a menace to his mother which would meet with her disapproval or with a withdrawal of her love. Therefore he cuts it off (hair=phallus) to please her, to retain her love. Similarly the reaction-formations are expressed in endeavours to keep the hair flat, tidy, etc., and perhaps most conspicuously in the ritual of shaving. We therefore become at peace with our various socialised parent-substitutes.

Reaction-formations against the anal component embodied in the symbolism are evidenced not only in this painstaking tidiness but more noticeably by the scenting to which we have already referred. I have had dream evidence to show that the custom of covering the hair with hat or other headdress is an expression of each side of the conflict. In so far as the hair is hidden it shows a fear of its exhibition, resulting in repression as a mental consequence and hiding as its behaviouristic equivalent. In so far as the headdress itself is exhibitionistic we have the positive impulses gratified by means of this displacement.

A patient dreamt that he was a soldier in uniform walking through the woodlands, with his helmet missing, and his hair blowing about in the breeze. He knew in consequence that his uniform was not in order. Eventually what he feared would happen did happen. He was arrested by the sergeant and forced to wear a blue badge to denote his misdemeanour. The curious interplay of castration elements and exhibitionistic elements was clearly revealed in his dream associations. The missing helmet was castration. The unruly hair was exhibitionism. Anxiety was present and was justified by the arrest. The blue badge had an association to gonorrhoea, which he had acquired through wearing a defective french letter from a blue envelope. This idea in the dream destroyed any doubt there might otherwise have been as to the phallic significance of his untidy hair-behaviour, and also (seeing that gonorrhoea was a castration) of the castration significance of his arrest.

Thus we see that our hair-behaviour is an expression of affect belonging to each side and every section of Oedipus, sexual and pre-genital, conflicts. It includes id resistance in the form of instinctive fear of the positive impulse, super-ego resistance in abundance (as exemplified by fear of parent-social-disapproval), and ego resistance, which last is shown by the various rational arguments brought forward to justify it.

### Id

Let us now consider what are the primitive instinctive sources from which our hair-activity obtains its dynamic force. It is repeatedly conspicuous that the hair is a genital symbol and it would appear that the instinctual level from which the displacement occurs is clearly genital (genital level of libidinal organisation). While endorsing this truth we will remember the abundant evidence that there are other instinctive factors to be discerned hiding behind the conspicuous genital symbolism as well as embodied within it.

### (a) Oedipus Organisation

To start from the higher, later levels of organisation and to work backwards : embodied within it we discern its object-relationship showing its derivation from the fully developed Oedipus Complex. Beneath the manifest adult behaviour of

87

suing for social approval of the hair or coiffure we can discern the little Oedipus suing for his mother's permission, approval or love of his genital sexuality. The anxiety attendant upon falling hair and baldness and the lavish expenditure on care and treatment of the hair may well be a measure of the anxiety attendant upon the early unconscious supplication. These facts should not surprise us if we remember that being observed, showing or exhibiting the phallus (or its physical and psychological equivalents), which is the first tentative step towards the supplication for approval, did not merely meet with frustration at its primitive level, but was displaced in some measure on to the hair. This has now clearly become a socially visible phallic-substitute, daily visible to all members of our social group (parent substitutes). What was at one time visible to the parents and disapproved (phallic-sexual frustration) is now in its substituted form (hair) being anxiously exhibited to society (parent-substitutes). Much hangs upon its acceptance. Let us remember in the perversion of exhibitionism the enormous amount of anxiety attendant upon the exhibitionist's performance. Let us correlate this with the anxiety about the appearance of our hair in response to which so much time and money is expended, and the great array of hairdressing establishments maintained. Is it less of a social cult now than it was when forming a part of the social-religious system of primitive people?

### (b) Anal

Hiding behind the phallic symbolism of hair we can detect signs of pre-genital component instincts. The association of hair with odours, either natural or artificial (perfumed sprays, lotions, oils, etc.) is well known. Who has visited the hairdresser without having to protest at, or meekly submit to, a restoration ritual in the form of scented spray! Tidiness, orderliness and cleanliness have been mentioned as anal reaction-formations. Libidinal components from the anal level come clearly out into the open in the clinical material from the last two patients quoted in Section VI of this book.

This material shows distinct, if sparse, evidence of positive libidinal urges emanating from this level : vide the patient who goes out of doors with sand (excrement) instead of hair or lather upon his face, his desire for the love-object's (mother's) venereal disease, dirt or faeces, his desire to have these anal qualities in himself approved or loved by the mother (by society). All this and its intimate connection with his exhibitionism has a pre-genital origin in his infantile desire that his mother should allow and appreciate his anal-erotic instincts and pleasures. The evidence from anthropological sources though amply confirmative of the genital level of libidinal impulse in hair symbolism is not so obvious in its anal undercurrent. Nevertheless we may detect in the leaving of bodily residue in the form of hair in tombs and as a sacrifice to deities[1] (parent representatives) a close analogy to the infant's surrender of its valued material to the loved parent. The erotic value of the smell of hair is also referred to by Havelock Ellis. As previously mentioned (*vide* footnote on page 79), Groddeck insists that falling in love depends unconsciously on the sense of smell (though no special reference is here made to hair). All this is not very surprising, as the patient last quoted in Section VI reminds us in unmistakable terms, of the anal origin of phallic erotism : 'the penis is only s—.'

## (c) *Aggression or Death Instinct*

But that is not the whole story of the positive instinctive drives that lend their energy to hair activities. We have said

[1]This paper. 'Anthropological Evidence', Section IV.

that they were clearly libidinal. And certain factors remind us that the aggressive impulse if not the primary destructive instinct is also here. Aggression, at least libidinised aggression or sadism, is conspicuous in the remarks of our last patient. May it not also be detected beneath the *reaction-formation* of the prevalent cutting, singeing and especially the shaving of our hair ? Is it not against our aggression rather than against an otherwise harmless phallus that we are directing insistently the sharp blade of the razor ? Do we not intuitively detect something of this objectionable quality (aggression) in our fellow man who has neglected to shave ? We feel that he is 'scruffy', dirty, anti-social, *aggressive*. (In psycho-analytical terminology : anal-sadistic.)

In shaving and hair-cutting we abreact our agression by directing it against our aggressive hair.

If it is granted that hair is conspicuously a genital symbol, and that our mental attitude towards hair and our activities with it are a displaced expression of our sexual conflict (largely at the genital level), the problem then arises as to why it is *hair* we have picked upon for the symbolic expression of this conflict.

The first answer one finds to this problem is merely that hair serves as a convenient and suitable symbolical object for the repressed tension of the unconscious conflict both at its genital and anal level. For example :

(1) Hair is freely admitted to consciousness ; indeed it cannot easily be ignored by consciousness.

(2) It is a part of us and yet not a part. It is detachable, removable, cutable, etc. We can innocently play with it. It is visible socially to our fellows.

(3) The sexual conflict is not limited to hair in its symbolic expression. A host of other objects can be, and are, freely chosen for its expression or relief. They are cathected by the unconscious in proportion to their convenience and representative ability ; e.g.

finger and toe nails, hats, shoes, clothes, umbrellas, sticks, purses, jewellery, etc. (objects detachable from our person). The process reminds us of that to which Freud alludes in describing dream-mechanisms.[1] Some *recent* object or experience is chosen to manifest the repressed latent thoughts. Hair is always with us —always recent.

In addition to these qualifications of hair to represent the genitals, as a more displaced and less censored symbol of sexuality, we have the fact that hair is a secondary sexual character in so far as it develops in special regions (the face, pubes, etc.) coincident with genital maturation.

### Id proper

Perhaps the true explanation of why hair should be singled out as a genital substitute *par excellence* is to be found in the hint previously given[2] that hair is a physical expression of (genital) libido :

'As a prototype of all the transformations to which the libido becomes subjected in the course of its long history . . . stags and lions grow antlers and *manes* (hair) in the rutting period *because the surplus of libidinal energy recedes back from the genital organ to the whole body.*'[3]

In the same way the surplus of libidinal energy at puberty recedes back from the genital organ to the whole body particularly to the pubes, and in males to lips and jaws where it reveals itself in the physical outgrowth of hair. Apart from puberty the hair of the body (e.g. head hair) may well be a similar diffuse physical expression of libido. Havelock Ellis points out that hairiness is commonly recognised as indicating sexual virility.[4] In confirmation of

[1]Freud : *The Interpretation of Dreams*, Chapter V.
[2]This paper, Section VI.
[3]Róheim : *The International Journal of Psycho-Analysis*, Vol. XIII, Parts 1 and 2, pp. 94-95
[4]Havelock Ellis : *Studies in the Psychology of Sex*, Vol. V, p. 196

G

this we have an example of the opposite in the patient who lost his hair (alopecia) when he was unconsciously convinced of castration. This is a common phenomenon of which many clinical psychologists have had experience. A large number of 'shell shock' cases (i.e. persons whose state of fear represented unconscious phantasy of castration or loss of life) suffered from alopecia sometimes amounting to complete baldness during the weeks of mental illness following their traumatic experience.

It appears that conventional hair-behaviour, the periodic hair cuttings, the daily hair brushings and *particularly the daily shave*, are a present-day ritual-*symptom* exactly analogous to many savage and ancient customs—for example, the subincision ceremony of the Arundas. It has been shown by Róheim[1] that the Arunda ceremony of subincision is a social symptom that serves the purpose of expressing dramatically their castration anxiety. In this symbolic fashion the cathexis of affect belonging to the castration complex is periodically abreacted thereby obviating the necessity for a characterological change. The only difference between this symptom and our modern hair ritual is that in the former the symbols used (penis and incision of penis) are, as one would expect in a primitive degree of culture, certainly not far removed from their anatomical source, indeed their phallic origin is patent, whereas in our modern practice displacement and disguise are so extreme that to the average person the disguise is effective. He will not discern (without being psycho-analysed) that in dealing with hair so remote as that of his face and head he is unconsciously dealing with a phallic substitute.

*Id* := He plays with and treasures this 'phallus' daily.

*Super-ego* := He controls (tidies), lays down, brushes flat,

[1] Róheim : *International Journal of Psycho-Analysis*, Vol. XIII, Parts 1 and 2, pp. 113 and 118

cuts off and shaves (castrates) this anti-social phallus.

*Ego* :—   He does what society expects of him and is none the worse for it except for the loss of time and the disadvantages enumerated in Section II. Indeed he feels better for it chiefly because he thus 'deals with' the conflict between Id and Super-ego without unduly embarrassing his ego—*that is to say by a symptom rather than by a character change.*

As Róheim says, the Arundas by their subincision ceremony cathect the castration complex and avoid character changes. A castration complex which was not cathected would produce character changes, that is, would achieve its cathexis in character modification.

We have no subincision ceremony but achieve similar results by our custom of shaving and hair-cutting.

All this may teach us nothing more than we have already suspected, namely, that our hair activities are but another substitutive expression of our sexual conflict—conspicuously a genital level of conflict, but with the usual contribution from the pre-genital component instincts. We have merely drawn attention to another habitual method of expression of well-known unconscious material.

This study will have served its purpose if it makes us realise once again the following truth, which is more or less strongly resisted by all in inverse proportion to their amount of psycho-analytical experience : that, in spite of apparent exceptions, an examination of *any* example of our behaviour reveals the fact that the unconscious mind is ever charged with the tensions of the unsolved Oedipus Complex and its pre-genital components (including anal-sadism and aggression) ; and that our behaviour whether we call it 'normal' or pathogenic, sublimation, substitution, play, or symptom, is essentially *an expression of the various opposed tensions of this unconscious conflict.*

We see ourselves preoccupied with our unconscious conflict : instinct drives (libidinal and aggressive) versus repressing forces. This conflict, as in the case of an obsessional patient, is displaced on to symbols. And in its new symbolic disguise it is played out again and again without ever reaching any hope of solution. Our 'normal' activities of everyday life consist largely of such 'obsessional' preoccupations. As we see in our insight into our activities with hair, we are repeating the unsolved struggle between instinct drives (genital and pre-genital) and the castrating efforts of the repressing forces, at the instigation particularly of the super-ego. The whole conflict has been displaced upwards to the socially visible hair of the head and face.

And so our preoccupation with the unsolved primitive past has found its way into our modern civilised life, in a form which, by virtue of its symbolism, ensures it against any likelihood of solution. We call this normality : to go on repeating our old struggles with obsessional persistence until death overtakes us and ends the matter with a final castration.

# Glossary

ABREACTION. The re-experiencing of repressed emotional tension.

AFFECT. The energy of an emotion. It may be aroused by a variety of stimuli and is capable of displacement on to concepts with which it was not originally associated.

ALOPECIA. Baldness.

AMNESIA. A memory blank.

ANAL EROTISM. Pleasurable sensations experienced through the act of defecation, or other stimulation of the anus, especially enjoyed in childhood and repressed later.

CASTRATION. Removal of the organs of generation.

CATHEXIS. A charge of emotional energy investing an idea or object.

COMPLEX. A group of affectively charged ideas which, through conflict, have become repressed into the unconscious.

CONFLICT. 'War' between opposing elements in the mind.

DEATH INSTINCT. According to Freud, a deeply-rooted instinctual impulse that serves to take the organism back as far as possible to its original inorganic state. It is supposed to be closely associated with destructive, aggressive and repetitive tendencies in the psyche, and to contrast with the 'life' or libidinal instinct.

DEFECATION. The act of discharging excreta from the anus.

DEFLORATION. The act of deprivation of virginity. The breaking of the hymen.

DETUMESCENCE. Subsidence from swelling. A term much used by Havelock Ellis to denote what he calls the second part of physiological sexual activity. The first part, tumescence or becoming tumid, is followed, with or without orgasm, by a comparatively rapid subsidence of the tumidity with decline in excitation.

DISPLACEMENT. The transfer of an affect from the idea to which it was originally attached to an associated idea. It is one of the most important unconscious mechanisms in the production of phobias and other symptoms.

EGO. That part of the id which has become modified by the impingement of external stimuli in such a way that it has become adapted to reality, reality testing and activity, and is credited with consciousness. In contra distinction to the id, it tends to organisation into a united whole.

EROTIC. Sexual.

EXHIBITIONISM. Displaying the penis or other part of the body or showing one's prowess in order to excite sexual interest.

FAMILIALLY. Pertaining to the family. (The word 'familial' does not appear in the *Oxford English Dictionary* though it is used in medical books, especially in neurology, and it occurs in *Psycho-Analysis Today*, pages 76 and 84.)

FECUNDATE. Impregnate.

FETISH. Anything which is attractive on account of its association, usually through unconscious elements, with erotic pleasure.

FIXATION. Arrest of a portion of the libidinal stream at an immature stage of development, either with reference to its erotogenic zone or with reference to its object attachment or both. The level of a fixation determines the type of any psychosis or psychoneurosis which later may occur, and the nature of its object attachment may determine its presenting form.

GENITAL ORGANISATION. That mature stage of libidinal development when the component instincts have become synthesised with genital primacy and full capacity for object love. In infancy it gives rise to the Oedipus complex and in later life to psychosexual union.

HETEROSEXUALITY. Love for or erotic interest in a person of the opposite sex, i.e., normal psychosexual development.

HOMOSEXUALITY. Sexual desire for a member of the same sex.

HYSTERIA. A psycho-neurotic disorder resulting from a conflict between the libido, including non-genital organisation thereof, and the ego or super ego, in which the libidinal drives are repressed and thus excluded from direct or conscious expression, and in which the unconscious repressed material later, through displacement and conversion, finds an outlet by an indirect somatic pathway and thus produces symptoms. Freud describes two principal varieties : (1) anxiety hysteria, in which the predominating symptom is anxiety but distinguishable from anxiety neurosis in that the aetiological factors are psychological (such as infantile sexual traumata) rather than physical (e.g., disturbances in the current sex life); and (2) conversion hysteria, in which the principal symptoms are physical (hysterical pains, paralyses, etc.). Fixation hysteria is a less important concept applied sometimes to cases where the form or locus of the symptom has been strongly determined by some external factor, e.g., by a wound or physical illness.

ID. The concept of an undifferentiated primitive mind containing only innate urges, instincts, desires and wishes without consciousness or any appreciation of reality, and apparently dominated by the pleasure principle. Unlike the ego it is not organised or integrated, so that contrary and incompatible urges can exist side by side in it without necessarily entering into conflict with one another.

INHIBITION. Restraint or frustration of an impulse by an opposing force, usually by an intra-psychic force. A frustration from within the psyche.

INSTINCTS. Innate patterns of discharge of tension.

INTROJECTION. A mental process by which one identifies himself with another person or object incorporating it into his ego system, so that the previous object cathexis is transferred to a portion of his ego and this brings about a profound change in the intra-psychic libidinal situation. It is a process of assimilation of the object and of feelings associated to it; whereas 'projection' is a process of dissimilation.

LIBIDO. The energy of the sexual instinct and of its psychosexual component instincts. It is subject to many vicissitudes. For example, it can become aim inhibited (i.e., orgasm inhibited) and undergo unlimited displacement, even on to the person's own ego (narcissism, self-love), asexual objects and abstract ideas.

MASTURBATION. The act of producing sexual feeling by manual manipulation of one's own genital organ or other erotogenic zone.

NARCISSISM. Love of oneself.

NEUROSIS. A functional nervous disorder. By some writers used to designate any psychogenic illness.

OEDIPUS COMPLEX. As in the play (Oedipus Rex) by Sophocles, and as in the Greek legend on which it is founded, the unconscious of man from which these dramatisations originated, has been shown by psycho-analysis to contain a repressed constellation comprising a desire to displace the parent of the same sex and to possess the parent of the opposite sex. It is something more powerful than common sense that comes into effective conflict with the Oedipus constellation. It is specifically fear of castration which causes total repression of these desires and phantasies. Amongst the evidences of this repression there are the normal horror of incest, intimacy with the very person with whom one had since birth or before birth been most intimate, and the normal tendency to dramatise the repressed constellation in actuality, through the mechanism of displacement, by marrying a person in the image of the repressed imago, and the persistence, at least in physical form, of repugnance for those in the image of the once hated or displaced parent. Inability to deal adequately in these normal ways with the energy of the repressed complex and consequent regression to fixations at pre-Oedipus levels of libidinal organisation, are the nuclear bases of psychoneurotic, characterological and mental disorders.

ORAL EROTISM. Erotic excitation from stimulation of the mouth or lips, the primary source of erotic feelings in babyhood and continuing in variable degree throughout life in spite of the acquisition of genital maturity with which it becomes associated, as evidenced by the phenomena of kissing and various habits and conversions.

ORGASM. The point at which erotic excitement reaches its acme and becomes involuntary. On the latter account it is suppressed by most persons in proportion to their prevailing anxiety and ill-health.

PERVERSION. Any sexual act the object or mechanism of which is both biologically unsound and socially disapproved. Perversions are usually the manifestation of a psychosexual component instinct in substitution for mature genital sexuality.

PHALLIC. Pertaining to the phallus, the erect penis or its image, worshipped in some religious systems as symbolising generative power in Nature.

PHOBIA. Morbid or unjustifiable fear, e.g., of some harmless object, activity or situation. It is unconsciously associated with some repressed and feared instinct desire.

POLYTHEISM. Belief in more than one god.

PROJECTION. The attributing to persons or things outside oneself of mental processes, affects, etc., that originated within one's own mind (and have been repressed), with relief of tension; common in varying degrees to all minds, with consequent impairment of their reality appreciation. It is very characteristic of paranoia.

RATIONALISATION. The attributing of reasons for judgments, ideas or actions which are otherwise (usually emotionally) determined.

REACTION FORMATION. A character trait, or its development, unconsciously designed to hold in check, conceal or contradict a tendency of an opposite kind. Thus obsessional cleanliness would be a reaction formation against repressed dirtying tendencies. Disgust, shame and morality are other reaction formations.

REPRESSION. The rejection from consciousness, by an unconscious mechanism, of mental material, concepts and affects, which are unwelcome. Analysis has shown that this material remains active, and dynamic in the unconscious, that the expenditure of repressing energy continues and that the repressed commonly re-emerges in altered forms such as symptoms.

SADISM. The achievement of erotic pleasure by victimising the sexual object, commonly by inflicting helplessness or pain upon him.

SECONDARY SEXUAL CHARACTERS include every feature or characteristic that differentiates the sexes other than the genitals (primary sexual character). For instance, differences in distribution of hair (e.g., beards), bodily contour, voice, etc.

SUBLIMATION. The process of deflecting libido from sexual aims to interests of a non-sexual and socially approved nature.

SUPER EGO. That part of the mental apparatus developed in early life by the mechanism of repressing frustrated impulses, such as aggression, and projecting them on the frustrators and subsequently introjecting them. Its function is largely to oppose the id, often unreasonably, and even to criticise and punish the ego if it tends to accept id demands. It is a sort of primitive unconscious conscience.

SUPER EGO RESISTANCE. Resistance to analytical progress and insight emanating from the super ego and due to the rigidity of the latter's formation. For instance, moral or religious values early implanted do not readily yield to the impingement of a more recently acquired reasoning. Nevertheless, though super ego resistance is usually the first resistance encountered during analytical work, modification of the super ego in the light of reason is usually the first fruits of analytical progress.

SURROGATE. The representation of a person in substitution for another and the assignation to him of the role properly or originally belonging to another person.

SYMBOLISM.  Substitution of sexual objects and aims by apparently non-sexual ones. On analysis the latter are discovered to stand for, or to symbolise the former.

TRANSFERENCE.  A displacement of any affect from one person to another. Specifically during analysis the affects originally felt during infancy for the parents become unconsciously displaced on to the person of the analyst so that the analysand feels towards him unjustifiable love and hate and has no insight into the phenomenon and its irrelevance.

UNCONSCIOUS.  A region of the psyche which contains mental processes and constellations which are ordinarily inaccessible to consciousness, commonly owing to the process of repression. The technique of mind analysis is specially designed to bring this unconscious material into consciousness by overcoming the resistances and repressing forces, as it is from the unconscious conflicts or complexes and their opposing forces or reaction formations that all symptoms emanate.

# Index

Medusa, 39
Meik, Vivian, 5
Melanesia, 73
  Melanesians, 74, 83
menopause, 16
menstruation, 40
Merlin, 33
Milton, 71
monks, 71, 76
Moses, 78

narcissism, 62, 85
  narcissistic, 64, 85
Neill, A. S., 16
neuroses, 44, 85
  neurotic, 16, 65
nightmares, 16
nuns, 71

object, 85
  object, love, 43, 44, 58, 64, 72, 89
  object, part, 59, 64
  object, phallic, 63
  object, sexual, 66
  object, substitutive, 63, 65
obsessional, 94
  obsessional case, 46
  obsessional nature, 49
  obsessional symptoms, 41
  obsessional worries, 49
odours, 79, 80, 88
  odours, sexual, 79
Oedipus, 86, 87, 88
  Oedipus complex, 85, 87, 93
  Oedipus desire, 15
  Oedipus guilt, 16
  Oedipus phantasy, 16, 38, 75
  Oedipus situation, 45
  Oedipus wishes, 86
oral erotic stage, 55
  oral level, 61

oral plane, 67
orgasm, 48

parents, 40, 55, 85, 87, 89
parent figure, 28, 41
  parent representatives, 89
  parent substitutes, 86, 88
Payne, Dr., 55
penis, 11, 12, 13, 14, 17, 18, 38, 46, 47, 48, 49, 51, 59, 60, 61, 64, 68, 70, 71, 73, 74, 75, 76, 77, 78, 79, 92
  penis faeces, 49
  penis imago, 63
  penis substitute, 70
people, primitive, 21
permanent waving, 5, 7
Perrault, 33, 35
perversion, 39, 42, 57, 58, 65, 88
phallic, 40, 63, 64, 87, 88, 89, 92
  phallic anxiety, 49
  phallic level, 61
  phallic symbol, 29, 36
  phallic symbolism, 28
  phallic substitute, 62, 88, 92
phallus, 19, 42, 59, 60, 67, 77, 78, 85, 86, 88, 90, 93
phantasy, 29, 41, 43, 55, 57, 58, 59, 92
phobia, 65
pigmentation, 69
Plant, 29
polytheism, 27
Pope's *The Rape of the Lock*, 37
potency, 29, 34, 46
  potent, 35, 45, 46
pre-genital, 42, 64, 67, 80, 88, 89, 94
pregnancy, 69
projected, 55, 64
  projection, 65
proverbs, 34

For Product Safety Concerns and Information please contact our EU
representative  GPSR@taylorandfrancis.com
Taylor & Francis Verlag GmbH, Kaufingerstraße 24, 80331 München, Germany